THE SPORTING ART OF
FRANKLIN B. VOSS

For my old friends Harriet and Ike

Peter Winants

Also by
Peter Winants

Jay Trump: A Steeplechasing Saga

Flatterer: The Story of a Steeplechase Champion

Steeplechasing: A Complete History of the Sport in North America

Foxhunting with Melvin Poe

THE SPORTING ART OF
FRANKLIN B. VOSS

Peter Winants

ECLIPSE
PRESS

Lexington, Kentucky

Library of Congress Control Number: 2004113199

ISBN 1-58150-120-X

Printed in Hong Kong
First Edition: July 2005

Distributed to the trade by
National Book Network
4720-A Boston Way, Lanham, MD 20706
1.800.462.6420

A Division of
Blood-Horse Publications
Publishers Since 1916

ECLIPSE
PRESS

Table of Contents

Chapter Five ~ Foxhunting

Chapter Six ~ Miscellaneous Subjects

Foreword

By the era of Franklin Brooke Voss, photography was well established and evolved, perfectly capable of recording with acuity and accuracy the world of sport and the horse. Nevertheless, it has long seemed to me that the image, the touch — almost the heartbeat — of the horse world and the countryside of Voss' era reside more in his paintings than in old photographs.

Voss implanted his own vision and personality into a painting, and yet he was always faithful to the appearance of specific horses and riders. In much the same way I think of Henry Stull as conveying the spirit of racing in the late 1800s and turn of the century, Voss created a lingering image for the era when his own artistry enjoyed its potency. (And, his jockeys were far more realistic that those awkward plastic men of Stull's rambunctious race scenes.)

Many sporting artists, Voss among them, challenge themselves on two planes. In a sense, they are what they paint and they paint what they are, and if they contrive to fool their audience, they will be found out. Yes, a painter with a knack for depicting the general shape of a horse, or a mountain lion, or a racing automobile, can please those elements of the public who have a passing knowledge, or curiosity, about those subjects. In the case of a sportsman painting for other sportsmen, though, the natural constituency can be a devilish critic.

It amounts to an unofficial badge of honor that Voss is accepted, even revered, by those who have lived and breathed and been uplifted by the scenes he so brazenly presumed to depict. ("Brazen" here is not pejorative, for surely every artist who looks at the world and thinks a bit of its soul can be reduced to canvas by his/her own talent and vision requires a foothold of egotism.) Voss lived in the world of foxhunting and racing, and he developed a masterful touch as well as a practiced eye.

While sporting artists are often regarded as somehow lesser than portrait painters, still-life specialists, landscape artists, and the like, those who not only paint scenes but do specific horse portraiture — and do it well — deserve better. Picasso, one would assume, was immune from any carping that "the second Demoiselle d'Avignon from the left doesn't look just like I remember her," whereas Voss could not slip any inaccuracies on his portrait of Discovery, for example, past his sporting owner, Alfred Vanderbilt, and the horse's many admirers.

As author Peter Winants points out elsewhere in this volume, the general style and scenes of Voss made comparisons to Alfred Munnings inevitable. I personally hold that no greater compliment to a sporting artist could be imagined than that he is compared with any degree of favor to Munnings, and Voss is one of the few whom I would personally give that status. Both gave you not only their vision, but also a complex mixture that seemed to fuse the soul of the artists with the soul of the scenery.

And what scenery the worlds of foxhunting, steeplechasing, and racing provide! One is reminded of sportsman Paul Mellon's delightful paean to the genre, in his case a specific celebration of England: "Newmarket beckoned me ... I still hark back to those long, soft, eminently green gallops stretching to the horizon in the slanting afternoon sun, and the late October sunlight on the warm yellow stone of the old, high stands ... the bright colors of the silks flashing by, the sheen of the horses' coats ..."

Among Munnings' devices in recording his own vision of such scenery was the splash of red, placed quite specifically on the canvas, a common trait among artists of other stripe as well. For John Constable, this might take the form of a lady's cloak as its wearer admires Salisbury Cathedral from a corner of the scene, or the shirt of a small lad reclining to drink directly from a brook, or perhaps the harness collar of a white horse on a barge. Childe Hassam found a similar opportunity in a rose dislodged from a lady's bouquet and lying on the road as an assemblage of grand carriages and formally attired swells sets out along the Champs-Élysées.

Racing — with its flags and bunting as well as lady's hats and jockey silks — provides ready opportunities for that touch of red. Voss, too, was adept at its use, perhaps a flag in the distance of a steeplechase course or a barn far off in the country. Foxhunting, of course, with its splendid red coats, presents all the red an artist could possibly want and nullifies the subtlety, whereas his series of portraits for Calumet Farm were provided with ready-made red, but not in such profusion. With the Calumet colors being devil red-and-blue, Voss made casually precise placements of red via water buckets, blankets, or gates in the distance.

Many of the twenty-three portraits in the Calumet series were of grand matrons, and yet the subjects' placements amid what *The New Yorker* once described as the "sexy" contours of the farm show the training track rail far in the distance, a suggestion of glories past and future for these distinguished mares and their foals. They are among Voss' most intimate presentations: Nellie Flag's fine chestnut muzzle and pinkish nose; the alertness and the dapples of Whirlaway's dam Dustwhirl; the sheen on the flank of Wistful. Perhaps in a conscious show of bravado, Voss even conquered the depth problem of showing a horse turning to look at the viewer. Nothing baffles photography of horses like the head being turned toward the camera, almost invariably creating an awkward impression of a heavy-headed animal even to the most expert cameraman or photographer. With Coaltown's dam, Easy Lass, Voss depicted this gesture without loss of her loveliness.

The work of a master, and a horseman.

That Franklin Voss has as his champion herein none other than Peter Winants is as tidy a fit as the red and blue on a Calumet water bucket. Winants, too, is as much horseman as observer and interpreter of horses and their world.

We first met when he and his brother, Garry, operated an equine photography business based in Baltimore. Winants Brothers was contracted by the weekly publication *The Blood-Horse* to cover the Triple Crown races each spring as well as various other assignments of track and farm. In the 1960s and 1970s, the weekly magazine was not produced until Wednesday. Thus, coverage of the Kentucky Derby, for example, meant a quick flight home for Peter and Garry that evening, a night in the studio printing black and whites, and a trip to the airport to express a packet of photos back to Lexington, Kentucky. When the Triple Crown stop was in Baltimore for the Preakness, the procedure was amended: A staff member had to stay in good enough shape through the post-race revelries to show up at Winants Brothers in the early morning hours and carry the package back on the flight the next morning. Well, the Triple Crown is *supposed* to be a test of stamina.

Peter liked to stand on the roof of the stands rather than in the press box to click off his sequence photos of the running of the races. This required a certain lack of concern over how close to the edge of the racetrack roof he had to be. I joined him once atop Belmont Park and was somewhat dismayed to note there was no railing inasmuch as it was not the intent that races be watched from that perch. While more than 80,000 were accommodated elsewhere on the grounds, Winants chose this unprotected aerie for his view of Canonero II's failed attempt at the Triple Crown in the Belmont Stakes. I stood somewhat meekly behind and, in later years, took the attitude that a member of the press belonged in the security of the press box.

This determination to get the best picture regardless of angle or contortion led Peter to disappear from view one day when we were working together on an article about one Dr. I.W. Frock. This low-budget but high-principled Marylander had constructed a sort of conveyor-and-trough approach to allow him to feed a great many horses himself, without having to hire much outside help. At one point, we looked around for the photographer and finally spotted him more or less dangling from the rafters of the weathered wooden barn. That vantage point provided the best view to illustrate how the system worked, so that was the vantage point Peter insisted on using.

The courage of his professional dedication was matched by the quality of his work. In those days, the 1960s, many of us even in the flush of youthful pride in our own employer's publication conceded that the most visually attractive of the Thoroughbred magazines was the monthly *The Maryland Horse*. Winants Brothers' photos proliferated in that publication and had a great deal to do with its overall tone and handsomeness.

Peter Winants, like Voss, grew up in the hunt fields, so his eye for a horse and the scene probably seems to come naturally to him. In truth, his was a finely developed craft.

Happily, in the next era of his career, Winants turned his attention to the written word as well as the recorded scene, as editor and later publisher of *The Chronicle of the Horse*. Later, the more academic aspects of racing history were his purview as he headed the National Sporting Library for a number of years before his retirement. In each of these fields — as had been true in photography — his adeptness grew, as witness his superb *Steeplechasing: A Complete History of the Sport in North America*. There was Peter Winants complete — horseman, photographer, historian, writer.

Now he is back to lend his talents to the rousing subject of the art of one he has long admired. Neither Voss nor the reader could have asked for more.

Edward L. Bowen
Versailles, Kentucky

Preface

The section in the stacks at the National Sporting Library devoted to sporting art is near the reference desk, easily accessible, which is proper because sporting art is one of the most popular segments of the collection for researchers and pleasure readers.

The books are shelved alphabetically by the artists' names: C.W. Anderson, Paul Brown, Lionel Edwards, Michael Lyne, George Ford Morris, Sir Alfred Munnings, Richard Stone Reeves, George Stubbs, and many more. In the V section, the name Voss was conspicuous by its absence; surprisingly, a book had never been written on the man many sporting art enthusiasts, including myself, feel is America's foremost equine painter of the twentieth century.

Three years ago I decided the omission should be righted, and I was confident that I was the one to do it. As I relate in Chapter One, I knew Frank Voss and was a friend and neighbor in Maryland of members of the Voss family. I am a longtime admirer of Voss' work — no less than thirty-five years ago I wrote an article on his art for *The Maryland Horse* magazine — and it is my privilege to own three of his paintings. Furthermore, my sporting interests are the same as Frank's: foxhunting, steeplechasing, and horses, horses, horses. I have a feel for his work, and I often react to his paintings by wishing I were in the painting, enjoying the fun.

Fortunately, the staff at Eclipse Press, a division of Blood-Horse Publications, shared my enthusiasm for a book on Voss, and we were off to the races. I established a game plan of writing an essay on the sporting and social significance of the subjects in each of the fifty-some paintings chosen. I selected paintings that excited me artistically,

of course, and those about which I either had firsthand knowledge of the subject or where research was available in the collections of the National Sporting Library and the Keeneland Association Library or in back issues of *The Blood-Horse*, *The Chronicle of the Horse*, and *The Maryland Horse* magazines.

Some of the paintings bring back memories of people such as Bryce Wing and Louise Bedford, who were my idols. Others are of horses I "knew," such as Seabiscuit, Whirlaway, Shut Out, Citation, and Hill Prince, and horses before my time such as Man o' War, Sir Barton, Gallant Fox, Equipoise, Billy Barton, and Alligator.

Many paintings in the book are of huntsmen, including quite a few that were good friends of my stepfather, Bryce Wing. As a youth I heard stories and looked up to sportsmen like Plunket Stewart, Watson Webb, Alex Higginson, Ambrose Clark, and Dean and Louise Bedford.

Some of the paintings show sport with the Elkridge-Harford Hunt, which was Frank's favorite hunt, and where I hunted as a child and young adult, sometimes with Frank. Pictures such as *The Swamp Fox*, *The Elkridge-Harford Hunt Crossing Atlanta Hall Meadow*, and *Dallas Leith's Hounds* bring back fond memories. In addition, Frank's versatility is indicated by the inclusion of associated subjects such as carriage driving, poultry, Norwich terriers, bassets, beagles, and children.

I'm confident that you'll enjoy Frank Voss' art, and I hope my text will give a feel of the era in which Voss worked (1912 until his death in 1953), a period many consider the heyday of American sporting life. I'm not going to get on the stump and insist that there's never been anything to equal "the good old days," but I will stump for the uniqueness of some of the happenings in my essays:

- For instance, the followers of the Meadow Brook (N.Y.) Hunt had the use of special rail cars that took them directly from New York City to special stops along the line on Long Island for meets of foxhounds;
- Liz Whitney hobnobbed with movie stars and named some racehorses in their honor, and Liz Taylor (the horse) was a stakes winner;
- Dr. A.C. Randolph, the longtime master of the Piedmont (Va.) Fox Hounds, gave up the birthing of babies and other mundane matters to concentrate on foxhunting; Mrs. Randolph once hunted thirty consecutive days until her streak ended for Christmas shopping;
- Man o' War ("de mostest hoss," according to groom Will Harbut) won twenty of twenty-one starts, carrying weights up to a crushing 138 pounds;
- Jockey Charlie Plumb (father of Olympic horseman J. Michael Plumb) remounted Alligator (our cover subject) after falling at the second fence in the 1929 Maryland Hunt Cup and went on to win in a field of fourteen horses, and he duplicated that feat to win the first running of the International Gold Cup in Tennessee in 1930;
- Shut Out, the Kentucky Derby winner in 1942, was well named in that his dam was Goose Egg and "goose eggs" or zeros on a baseball scoreboard equal a shut out.
- Hill Prince — a national champion at two, three, and four — was produced from Hildene, whom Christopher T. Chenery had purchased for $750, and sired by Princequillo, who at the time stood for a $250 stud fee.

History is fun. Almost as much fun as Frank Voss' art. Share my enthusiasm.

Peter Winants
Rectortown, Virginia
January 2005

Chapter One

A Family of Artists

Frank Voss' father, William, moved from Baltimore to Hewlett, Long Island, shortly after the Civil War for a career in banking and real estate. Born in 1880, Frank was the fourth of William's six children.

Frank Voss' sister, Jessie Lewis, a prominent portrait artist, did this pastel of their mother, the former Caroline Kane Neilson.

Many consider Franklin Brooke Voss, who died in 1953 at the age of seventy-three, the finest American equine artist of the twentieth century, and some go a step further, labeling him the best ever. Voss had a natural affinity for his subject matter, for he practiced what he painted. A consummate sportsman, Voss was equally at home riding to hounds and attending the races as he was working behind the easel.

Voss' love and admiration for the equestrian way of life were deeply rooted in his Virginia heritage even though he was New York-born and -raised. He was descended from Edward Voss, who emigrated from Wales to Virginia in the mid-1700s. Frank's great-grandfather, Robert Brooke Voss (1765–1811), lived on the family homestead, Mountain Prospect, near Culpeper, Virginia. His grandfather, Benjamin Franklin Voss (1800–1886), lived in Falmouth, Virginia, but moved to Baltimore prior to the Civil War. One of his eight children, Franklin, lost his life in that war.

Another son, William, moved from Baltimore to New York shortly after the Civil War to pursue a career in banking and, later, real estate. In 1878 he became one of the founders of the Rockaway Hunt at Cedarhurst on the south shore of Long Island and served as the club's treasurer from 1878 to 1884. William's brother, Joseph, remained in Maryland and co-founded, also in 1878, the Elkridge Hounds.

William H. Voss and his wife, the former Caroline Kane Neilson, had six children: William, known as Neilson (1876); Jessie (1878); Caroline (1879, died at age six); Frank (1880); Edward, known as Ned (1883); and Stuart (1885). The senior Voss died in 1928 at the family home, Merrifield, near Hewlett, Long Island.

Frank Voss enthusiastically accepted his family's lifestyle, becoming an avid horseman. In Frank's youth the Rockaway Hunt Club not only offered foxhunting but also had a major steeplechase meet, pigeon shooting, cockfighting, polo, tennis, and golf. In 1882 Rockaway became one of the first clubs in America to have polo matches, and in 1894 Rockaway hosted the Great Long Island Steeplechase, the American version of the English Grand National because of its huge fences. Harry Harwood, a regular foxhunter with Joseph Voss' Elkridge Hounds, ventured north to win the big race on Tonkaway. Steeplechasing remained popular at Rockaway until 1938 when the sport became a victim of the Great Depression.

Frank foxhunted as a child and later rode in steeplechase races and played polo. He also enjoyed hunting with Meadow Brook Hunt's drag pack on the north shore of Long Island, where stiff post-and-rail

HISTORY REPEATS

Frank Voss' father, William, and Louis Neilson, who were among the founders of the Rockaway Hunt Club on Long Island in 1878, were related, in that William Voss married Caroline Kane Neilson, a cousin of Louis Neilson. Both of the founders also share the distinction of having descendants who are prominent sportsmen. Neilson is the father of Louis (Pat) Neilson Jr., who was a master of foxhounds and once rode in the Maryland Hunt Cup, and the grandfather of Louis (Paddy) Neilson III, who rode in twenty Maryland Hunt Cups and won three. Paddy's daughter Sanna Hendriks won the Maryland Hunt Cup twice and was the first female rider to win the Virginia Gold Cup. She is one of America's leading steeplechase trainers, and her sister Katherine Neilson is likewise a successful trainer. Katherine saddled Young Dubliner to win important races over timber, including the 2003 Maryland Hunt Cup. Rockaway, the name of Paddy Neilson's farm in Pennsylvania, reflects Paddy's pride in his heritage. He and his wife, Toinette, who also rode in steeplechase races with great success, train horses at Rockaway Farm, and their daughter, Emily, rides in pony races.

William Voss' son Ned (Frank's brother) was master of the Elkridge-Harford Hunt in Maryland for thirty-four years. Ned's grandson, Tom Voss, has been champion steeplechase trainer in America four times through 2004 while training horses at Atlanta Hall Farm. Tom has also followed in his grandfather's footsteps as a joint-master of the Elkridge-Harford Hunt.

Through marriage, the Voss family is related to the Elder and White families of Maryland; both have members that have been prominent in sport and art. Frank's first cousins, Robert North Elder Jr. and George Elder, rode winners of the Maryland Hunt Cup in the late 1800s; William Voss Elder was curator at the White House under the Kennedys and curator of decorative arts at the Baltimore Museum of Art. Frank's cousin, Charles R. White, won the 1934 Maryland Hunt Cup, and White's sister, Suzanne White Whitman, was head of the riding department at Garrison Forest School in Maryland for thirty years. Champion steeplechase rider A. Patrick (Paddy) Smithwick was Mrs. Whitman's son-in-law; her grandson, Patrick Smithwick, was second and fourth in the Maryland Hunt Cup on horses trained by Tom Voss.

PHOTOGRAPH BY UNIVERSAL, COURTESY OF MID-ATLANTIC THOROUGHBRED

Frank Voss was photographed in 1926 while foxhunting in England with the Duke of Beaufort's hounds.

Elsa Horne Voss, who was married to Frank Voss' brother, Ned, created splendid bronzes of horses and other animals. Her Morning Gallop *is in the collection of Mr. and Mrs. Thomas H. Voss.*

Edward S. (Ned) Voss worked mostly in watercolors. His cowboy study, in the collection of Mr. and Mrs. Thomas H. Voss, was done at the Voss ranch near Sheridan, Wyoming.

fences, ranging up to five feet high, were frequently encountered at a racing pace.

In his teens Frank displayed his artistic talent. Pencil doodlings, often in the margins of schoolbooks, captured hunting and racing scenes. Rather than attend college, Frank studied for seven years at New York's Art Students League, which was founded in 1875 and as of 2004 remains an important center for art education. Frank's mentor was George Bridgman, a legendary instructor who wrote *Constructive Anatomy*, *The Human Machine*, and other books that remain valuable for art students. Frank also studied for a time in Paris.

With such a thorough art education, Frank Voss could have expressed himself in many fields. He chose, however, to combine his lifelong avocation of horses with his vocation in art. He first painted family members; his picture of brother Ned is on page 25; his father, on page 85. In no time, fellow devotees of horses and sport turned to him, first on Long Island, then throughout hot beds of sport in various areas.

Jessie, Stuart, and Ned shared in varying degrees their brother's artistic skills. Jessie, who worked mostly in pastels in her studio in New York, became one of America's most acclaimed portrait artists. Stuart made light of his talents in an interview in *The Maryland Horse* in 1971: "During Prohibition, I painted figures of horses and hunting on the labels of liquor bottles obtained by friends from moonshiners." Stuart also sometimes picked up scissors and from pieces of paper cut remarkably detailed silhouettes of hunting scenes and horses and carriages. Ned Voss enjoyed working in watercolors and oils. Prints of his watercolor, *The Harford Fox*, are in demand by collectors, as are his pictures of a meet at St. James Church and hunting scenes across his Atlanta Hall Farm.

Stuart said that the Voss children didn't inherit artistic talent from their father's side of the family. "Mother, though, was a Neilson, and the Neilsons were artistic; we must've gotten it from them," he said. A cousin, Raymond P.R. Neilson (1881–1964) did portraits of sportsmen, and he also painted horses and gun dogs. His painting of J. Watson Webb, the master of the Shelburne Hounds and a president of the Masters of Foxhounds Association of America, hangs at the Shelburne Museum in Vermont; his painting of sportsman F. Ambrose Clark (page 17) is in the National Museum of Racing and Hall of Fame, Saratoga Springs, New York.

However, no member of the Voss/Neilson family could match Frank's productivity and reputation in art. In a career that stretched from 1912 to 1953, he completed at least five hundred commissions.

"He was the finest equine painter in America in the twentieth century, the equivalent here of Sir Alfred Munnings in England," said F. Turner Reuter Jr., the proprietor of Red Fox Fine Art in Middleburg, Virginia. "Not only was he a brilliant animal painter who clearly understood animal anatomy, but he also was a wonderful landscape painter whose canvases spoke to the soul of country life with their colors, buildings, fences, grasses, skies, and trees. Voss, too, was a master with the human form. Again, he knew it intimately. Boots and breeches, for example, looked as if they were worn over real legs, and his humans had heads, shoulders, and hands that worked on real bodies under smart clothes. There is life, movement, and attitude in Voss' work."

Frank Voss' client list (see his Book of Orders, 1912–1922, in the Appendix) reads like a Who's Who of notable sportsmen of the golden days. His subjects included legendary racehorses such as Man o' War, Equipoise, Seabiscuit, Sir Barton, Citation, and Whirlaway. In 1934 a set of ten hand-colored prints of famous racehorses, after paintings by Voss, sold for $250 for the set, $30 for a single print. Today, individual prints from this set, when rarely on the market, sell for a thousand dollars and more.

Voss' foxhunting pictures are even more prolific. He painted the staff and hounds of famous hunts like the Meadow Brook Hunt, Mr. Stewart's Cheshire Foxhounds, and the Elkridge-Harford Hunt, as well as countless pictures of foxhunters and hunting families throughout the United States. "Foxhunting Across America," a set of four prints from his paintings, published by Derrydale Press, is prized by collectors.

Most of Voss' paintings remain in private collections, handed down from one generation to another. Twelve of his paintings are in the National Museum of Racing, and the International Museum of the Horse at the Kentucky Horse Park in Lexington has twenty-three paintings that Voss did for Calumet Farm. Between 1947 and the present, thirty-eight of Voss' paintings have appeared on the cover of *The Chronicle of the Horse* magazine (see Appendix), an honor highly sought by artists, most of whom would settle for one or two covers.

In 1926 Frank accepted the Duke of Beaufort's invitation to hunt in England. There he painted a lovely picture of the Duke's hounds and staff in front of Badminton House, the site of the famous three-day event. The Duke thought so highly of the painting that he had Arthur Ackerman & Son of London make a private edition of one hundred prints as house presents for guests. This was the first of seven privately published lithographs and hand-colored aquatints made from the Badminton painting.

Raymond P.R. Neilson, Frank Voss' cousin, was a well-known portrait artist, and he also painted dogs and horses. The above portrait is of F. Ambrose Clark.

Frank Voss and his sister-in-law, Elsa Horne Voss, were members of a prominent family of artists.

Frank Voss puts the finishing touches on a portrait of Calumet Farm's Pensive, the 1944 Kentucky Derby winner. Twenty-three portraits that Voss did for Calumet are on permanent display at the International Museum of the Horse in Lexington, Kentucky.

This recognition paved the way for additional commissions in England. As a result, Voss is one of the few American artists listed in *The Dictionary of British Equestrian Artists*, an important treatise compiled in 1985 by Sally Mitchell, an equestrienne and dealer in sporting art in England.

While in England, Frank became a friend of Sir Alfred Munnings. It is said that Munnings told Voss, "We have a cinch. People who know horses don't know art, and people who know art don't know horses."

By the 1930s excessive urbanization threatened the Voss family's beloved sport of foxhunting on Long Island. Ned Voss had served as master of the Smithtown Hunt on Long Island from 1932 to 1935 and ridden regularly, too, with Meadow Brook. But soon he and other New Yorkers — including the author's stepfather, S. Bryce Wing — were looking to Maryland to acquire farms.

Ned Voss purchased Atlanta Hall Farm from Tim Durant, a colorful amateur steeplechase rider who twice rode in the English Grand National in the 1960s when he was in his sixties. Durant fell in the 1966 race, and in the 1967 version, he remounted, after falling, to finish last but in so doing was greeted with a rousing ovation for his pluck.

After World War II, Frank, Stuart, and Jessie followed Ned and his wife Elsa, whom he had married in 1922, to Maryland. By then Stuart was divorced from his Russian-born wife, Nina Trosava, and Jessie's husband, Daingerfield Lewis, had passed away. Frank was a lifelong bachelor. The siblings shared a house and studio a stone's throw from the Elkridge-Harford Hunt Club.

On January 31, 1953, Elkridge-Harford's pack pushed a good-running fox across a hill on Hope Farm, adjacent to Hess Road in some of the best foxhunting country in Maryland, or in the United States for that matter. Frank Voss had visited and enjoyed hunting throughout America and England, so he'd been treated to some incredibly beautiful areas. However, he often stated that the view from this hilltop was his favorite. Atlanta Hall Farm was in the distance across rolling countryside; historic St. James Church on My Lady's Manor was a short way west; and Frank's own place was just beyond Atlanta Hall.

But on this day the hunt came to a sudden end. As he was crossing the hill at Hope Farm on Maritime, his gray hunter, Frank Voss fell dead to the ground, a victim of a heart attack. Not surprisingly,

SOME PERSONAL MEMORIES

The members of the Voss family were among my parents' closest friends. Eddie Voss, Ned's son, was a contemporary of my brother Garry and me, as were Paddy and Mikey Smithwick, who lived in a bungalow at the Hunt Club, where their father, Alfred, a native of Ireland, was honorary huntsman. The Smithwick brothers went on to become members of the Racing Hall of Fame — Paddy as a steeplechase jockey, Mikey as a trainer. Sadly, Eddie died of a stroke at age thirty-nine.

As youngsters, the Voss/Smithwick/Winants gang sometimes flippantly gave nicknames to our elders. We referred to Frank Voss as "Swanky Franky," because he was short in build with a mustache, usually with a pipe clamped between his teeth, meticulous in dress, truly a dapper figure. Ned Voss earned the nickname of "The Bossman" because, as the longtime master of Elkridge-Harford (1935–1969), he was truly the boss, as he was in many other matters. However, I vividly remember Pearl Harbor Day, December 7, 1941. That day, Eddie, Garry, and I borrowed without permission — none of us had a driver's license — The Bossman's pick-up truck for some kind of adventure and managed to get it stuck in a ditch. We walked back to Atlanta Hall Farm, heads bowed, fully expecting The Bossman's wrath. Not so, for just then the news of Pearl Harbor came over the radio, and Mr. Voss couldn't have cared less about our problem.

Ned's wife, Elsa, was loved by all, young and old. She was down-to-earth and fond of the West (they had a ranch in Sheridan, Wyoming) and western music. She had a deep, wonderful laugh, a trait inherited by Eddie and passed on to Eddie's son, Tom, a well-known trainer of steeplechase horses.

The humane treatment of animals was a high priority for Elsa Voss. She was the founder and benefactress of the animal shelter in Harford County, Maryland. She also had amazing talent as a sculptress. From her studio at Atlanta Hall, she produced marvelous bronzes, mostly of horses. The majority of her work is in private collections. I can recall my parents saying that it was a shame that Elsa didn't have to do bronzes for a living, rather than just when the spirit moved, for she had as much talent in her way as Frank. Kathleen Beer, the late art dealer, said: "Mrs. Voss' artistry is true to the medium … Her horses are especially well observed, very correct."

The Bossman did my family a huge favor. As newlyweds in the early 1960s, my wife and I wanted to live in the Elkridge-Harford hunting country but couldn't afford it. He sold us for a song ($25,000, actually) a lovely house and barn on five acres at the northern boundary of his property, where we lived until moving to Virginia in 1972.

I inherited four paintings by Frank Voss upon the death of my stepfather, Bryce Wing, in 1975. A reproduction of my painting of Alligator, the winner of the 1929 Maryland Hunt Cup, is on the dust jacket of this book and on page 69. I also have prints of two of Frank's paintings, *The Elkridge-Harford Hunt Crossing Atlanta Hall Meadow* and *Tally-Ho*, as well as four prints of watercolors by Ned Voss. The immense pleasure of living with this art, combined with marvelous childhood memories of the Voss family, motivated me to undertake this book.

his death prompted the cliché of doing what you love best at the time of death, and, in Frank's case, the addition of dying at the exact spot in the countryside that he most loved.

Frank's sister, Jessie Lewis, stated in an article in *The Maryland Horse* that Frank, seventy-three at the time, had had a premonition about his death, that he spoke as follows at breakfast on the morning he died:

My eyes are getting bad. Suppose they go and I can't paint or foxhunt? I got a letter the other day from the Duke of Beaufort, who said that a friend had dropped dead in the hunting field. He was buried in his hunting clothes, and at the grave they blew 'gone away.' You know, I envy him.

Chapter Two

Critical Analysis

Franklin B. Voss is at work at an undisclosed site.

Frank Voss' studio at Monkton, Maryland, following the artist's death in 1953. Many of the pictures on the wall are sketches, or studies on canvas, from which final paintings were made.

Believe me, in addition to being a lifelong friend of the Voss family, there are other reasons why I am so enthusiastic about the art of Frank Voss. I've been involved in foxhunting and horse racing since childhood, so when I see one of Frank's pictures, I almost feel like I'm in it or wish I were. For instance, *Tally-Ho* (page 95) truly awes me. It's of Bryce Wing, his cap raised, sighting a fox in the Millbrook country of New York, a scene every foxhunter craves. When hounds were established on the line (had the fox scented), I'm certain that he cut loose with a tally-ho that was heard all over the countryside. What a voice he had. What a thrill for the members of the field, who are shown coming into view at the right side of the canvas. What a thrill for me or any other foxhunter to view the painting.

I was a professional photographer for twenty years, specializing in advertising portraits of horses and scenes of foxhunting and horse racing. I quickly caught on that a good picture needs depth. How about the depth in *Tally-Ho*? Bryce Wing and the fox are in the foreground; staff and hounds, in the center. Several trees are on the right and a thicket of trees is in the middle distance on the left, leading the eye to the delightful countryside that rolls away to the horizon.

And there's nothing one-dimensional, either, about the painting of Alligator on the cover and on page 69. Brilliant sunlight highlights Alligator's coat. The trainer and jockey are in partial shade so as not to divert attention from the subject. The post-and-rail fence adds a touch of depth, and the branches of the stately oak frame the subject. The steeplechase fence and a handful of spectators on the upper right side of the canvas add to the depth, and the woods, in subtle fall foliage, form a final backdrop. The painting was done at the Meadow Brook racecourse on the estate of F. Ambrose Clark in Old Westbury, New York, where Alligator won the Meadow Brook Cup in 1928.

When in art school, Voss used family members as guinea pigs, as in his pictures of his father (page 85) and his brother Ned (page 25). Both date to 1905 and both lack detailed backgrounds and depth. Compare these to Voss' 1920 portrait of The Porter (page 37), where the landscape is tremendously attractive and a real asset to the painting. Obviously, Voss had gained confidence.

Thanksgiving Day Meet in 1923 of the Meadow Brook Hunt (page 107) is truly Voss' breakthrough painting. It is realistic in style and the composition flows. A huntsman and hounds are walking into

Frank Voss' montage of a cousin, Robert North Elder of Maryland, was done in 1902, when the artist, twenty-two, was a student at the Art Students League in New York City.

the canvas from the left; a gentleman is greeting a lady in the right center; a man in a pink coat is chatting with a lady in the right foreground; the Georgian mansion makes a marvelous backdrop. With this painting, Voss has come of age, having established his skill to capture animals and people in lovely landscapes. These talents came together time and again in his art, especially in his 1944 canvas of foxhounds over a coop (page 97), which is one of my favorite Voss paintings.

As leading contemporary sporting artists, Munnings and Voss are inevitably compared. To me, that's like comparing apples and oranges. To a large extent Munnings was able to paint things of his own choosing. Early on there were scenes of gypsies, horse fairs, and impressionistic landscapes and portraits. Later he produced delightful scenes of racehorses being saddled, going to the post, and breaking at the start. These paintings are marvelous; I love them.

Voss, on the other hand, was a commission painter from the start of his career. The first entries in his Book of Orders in 1912 were for Mrs. R.T. Wilson in North Carolina for a chestnut horse ($200), a fox terrier ($75), a pointer ($125), two pointers ($200), and three fox terriers ($200). You can rest assured that requests resulted such as "My horse, just like the one you did for Mrs. Wilson," or "My terrier, just like …"

So Voss, unlike Munnings, wasn't afforded the chance as a professional of doing pictures for sheer artistic expression, which is a shame. However, there is no indication that Voss regretted not having this freedom as a painter, and don't think for a minute that he didn't lead a great life. I remember my stepfather saying, "Frank's constantly on the go to pretty places all over. The right people are his hosts and clients. He eats their food, hunts their horses, paints them, and is well paid. He's never had it so good."

You can be sure, though, that in reality it was hard, tedious work. Voss' technique was to paint from life, not from photographs, a practice followed by many artists. He set up his easel on location, at the farm or racetrack, and made separate studies on canvas of the horse, the landscape, and the rider, if one was included. He then returned to his studio and combined the studies into a finished painting. Many of these studies have found their way into private collections.

Voss once said: "I paint what I see. I view myself as an animal painter with horses as the prime interest. I put in the faults as well as the good points. I don't make any attempt to 'pretty up' a horse."

The following art experts comment on Voss and his painting, validating his worth as an important sporting artist.

Lori A. Fisher
Curator of Collections, National Museum of Racing and Hall of Fame

When the National Museum of Racing and Hall of Fame moved into its permanent home in 1955, many artifacts were donated to help establish the collections of the new museum. One of the first donations was a painting of Blue Larkspur by Franklin B. Voss, presented by his brother, Edward S. Voss. Two other Franklin Voss paintings were soon to follow that same year. These early donations indicate that within two years of his death, Franklin Voss was considered to be an important American sporting artist worthy of inclusion in the new national museum dedicated to the history of Thoroughbred racing. Today, the museum is fortunate to own twelve paintings by Franklin Voss.

The ability of Franklin Voss to capture the conformation and beauty of the Thoroughbred is reason enough for many racing enthusiasts to hold him in high esteem. But his achievements are even more meaningful when the breadth of his work is considered in conjunction with the artistic achievements of his other family members. The Voss family has long been a leader in steeplechasing and foxhunting, both on Long Island and Maryland. Not only did they participate in these sports during the first half of the twentieth century, but they also uniquely documented these events, along with the people and horses that participated, through various art media. Amazingly, all five of the Voss siblings, and one spouse, became artists.

Walta M. Warren
Artist and former curator, National Sporting Library

Voss' academic background in art enables viewers to share the feeling of being in, or wishing to be in, his paintings. Here is a painter who mastered the skill of offering a visual tour through, and into, the depicted landscape. These wanderings are defined in much the same way that Renaissance painters guided the eye of the viewer into the

Early on, Frank Voss used family members as guinea pigs. The portrait of his brother, Edward S. (Ned) Voss, done in 1905, shows stiffness in horse and rider, and the landscape lacks the depth and detail found in Frank's later work. This portrait is in the collection of Mr. and Mrs. Thomas H. Voss.

As a youngster, Frank Voss often sketched horses and sports in the margins of his school notebooks.

A photograph of Voss, surrounded by foxhunting scenes, was done in 1900, when the artist was twenty.

distance by offering a single footpath or perhaps the line of a meandering stream. Along the way, the viewer is given various opportunities to contemplate a point of interest before proceeding, often lured or even pushed forward with an enticing use of aerial perspective. Voss used an intricate series of diagonal planes defined by fence rows, tree-lined stream beds, distant hillsides, and variety of coloration and texture of brushstroke in the foreground to achieve a similar path into the picture plane.

The landscapes as well as the participants in Voss' paintings are bathed in an even distribution of clear, muted light. Images in the distance are seen in the same clear detail as those occupying the middle ground and the foreground. Originating in early Chinese scroll paintings, this 'flying bird' perspective provides the viewer a trail to follow as well as spots in which to linger, ponder, and enjoy before proceeding into the painting.

Peter L. Villa
Proprietor of Peter L. Villa Fine Art, New York City

My profession as a dealer of fine art was certainly inspired in some part by my early exposure to Frank Voss' paintings. Voss first painted a favorite beagle for my grandfather, Richard V.N. Gambrill, in 1915. Two years later he was a member of my grandparents' wedding party, and a lifelong friendship ensued. Over the course of the next thirty years, Voss demonstrated his artistic skills and versatility, painting numerous portraits of family members, their dogs, prized horses, and hounds. These subjects were well captured and usually portrayed in the local New Jersey landscape with recognizable architecture in the background.

In the 1920s and 1930s the greatest equestrian sportsmen in America formed an elegant and close-knit community. Foxhunting, racing, polo, and coaching were undertaken with great enthusiasm and high standards. Frank Voss created a unique visual history of this segment of American life. An accomplished sportsman himself, he had a gift of combining a sure and perfect knowledge of animal anatomy with a rare sense of artistry. Many of his commissioned works still remain with the families for which they were

Frank Voss often made studies of various components of a portrait.
The study of jockey Red Pollard, which is in the collection of Henry Pitts, was made for the painting of Seabiscuit on page 51.

At age fifteen, Frank Voss, a lifelong foxhunter, portrayed his favorite sport.

painted. When a larger collecting public comes to know his art, Voss' accomplishments will certainly be more widely appreciated and recognized.

Richard Stone Reeves
American equine artist

From an article by Laura Rose in the National Sporting Library's newsletter in the fall of 1998. Reeves was beginning his career in the early 1950s, during Voss' final days. One day the young artist watched as Voss worked on a portrait of Turf great Citation:

When I got to the barn, Voss was already working on Citation. He'd sketched out a drawing on canvas before he went to see the horse, and then he set up his easel and painted right there. Of course, racing was much more leisurely back then. In those days, there were lots of wealthy owners with their own trainers, and the trainer would allow the artist perhaps not all the time, but a lot of the time he needed. We can't do that now. These days, with insurance, lots of trainers won't allow the horse out for more than ten or fifteen minutes at a time ... I credit Voss' success to two factors: a strong art education and just plain natural talent. There were more good painters then: Munnings, George Ford Morris, Voss, Stainforth. They all had the same background — you learn the foundation in art school and then formulate the technique. Voss had great technique. He also had very good taste and a flair, which a lot of the other painters didn't.

F. Turner Reuter Jr.
Proprietor of Red Fox Fine Art, Middleburg, Virginia

From an article for the catalog of the Voss exhibit at the Museum of Hounds and Hunting in 1999:

In 1926 Voss made his first of many regular visits to England, where he met and hunted with the Duke of Beaufort, painted for private clients, and met A. J. Munnings, two years his senior. These artists undoubtedly spoke about their trade. Both used similar techniques of preliminary sketches, some in pencil, some in pen and ink and some in oils, developing a series of foundations, building for the final work. Munnings, however, was more free and loose, like his American mentor, John Singer Sargent, unlike Voss, who remained more painterly and academic ... Imagine, as a beginning, an artist standing in front of an easel, with brushes and a palette in hand, facing a blank white canvas. Then imagine an ending, the finishing of a painting of presence, depth, and quality, to most of us a daunting image, but to Frank Voss, the image was his raison d'etre.

Kathleen Beer
The late proprietor of Beresford Gallery

From an article by the author in *The Chronicle of the Horse*, September 18, 1992:

He painted like a real horseman. He was doing what he knew. He had a keen eye and breathed life into subjects. You can feel the emotion and the emotional state. When I visit the National Museum of Racing and see Voss' work side-by-side with other great artists, it convinces me that he holds his own, and then some, with anybody's art … Most of his paintings were commissions. Most are still family held. Occasionally, one slips out for sale or auction, but it's rare. When they start coming on the market — perhaps in the next generation — the market price, which is largely determined by auction prices, will skyrocket.

Larry Wheeler
Contemporary artist specializing in horse subjects

From an article by the author in *The Chronicle of the Horse*, September 18, 1992. Wheeler was an instructor at the Maryland Institute of Art and a conservator at the National Portrait Gallery and the Corcoran Gallery:

Voss' paintings often develop a network of cracks in the aging and settling of the paint. *Craquelure*, the French term for the condition, has nothing to do with Voss' artistic merit. It was a problem with many painters of his time. It was their technique to paint over many sittings, to paint heavily, layer on top of layer of paint, with many changes. The paints, then, built up so thickly that the chance of cracking resulted. Skilled craftsmen in art conservation can remedy the situation. Simply put, a wax adhesive is applied in hot liquid to the rear of the canvas. When pressure is applied, the cracked paints are pulled back to the plane of the canvas, and the wax adhesive holds them in place.

John Fairley
British art critic

From his book *The Art of the Horse*:

Voss' work has a rich and silken quality that gives the horses he paints a luxurious, pampered look.

E.J. Rousack
American art critic

From *The F. Ambrose Clark Collection of Sporting Paintings*:

At a very early age, with precocious ease, Voss started drawing and sketching. There was hardly a schoolbook of his that was not covered with horses and dogs. He was raised in an environment in which horses and hounds played an important part … He had an exceptional opportunity to observe and study horses in action … He had the gift of combining his knowledge of animal anatomy with a rare sense of artistry.

Eve P. Fout
Equine artist and founding member of the American Academy of Equine Art

When I commenced expressing a serious interest in art as a teenager, my parents suggested seeking advice from their friend Frank Voss. I traveled from Virginia to Voss' studio in Maryland. He was great, giving me his time and advice, and he encouraged me to seek the best instruction available in the basics, especially animal anatomy. Later, when studying art in New York, I spent time with Richard Stone Reeves and Paul Brown. Both were approachable, so helpful. After I was established as an artist, I, too, was able to help young, aspiring artists as one of the founding members of the American Academy of Equine Art, which offers exhibits of work by members and instructional workshops.

Chapter Three

Flat Racing

egions of fans dubbed him "Big Red," beloved stud groom Will Harbut described him as "de mostest hoss," and a poll by *The Blood-Horse* magazine named Man o' War the greatest horse of the twentieth century over Secretariat and Citation.

August Belmont II bred Man o' War in Kentucky. A foal of 1917, he was by Fair Play out of Mahubah, by Rock Sand. The name of Man o' War's dam gave an inkling that something good was in store, Mahubah meaning in Arabic "good greetings, good fortune."

Man o' War's breeder, however, didn't share in the good fortune. At the time, Belmont was a major in the U.S. Army in Spain and decided to cut down on his horse interests back home. As a result, he consigned Man o' War to the yearling sales at Saratoga. Samuel D. Riddle, then lightly involved in horse racing but a veteran horseman and foxhunter, the master of the Rose Tree Hunt in Pennsylvania, purchased Man o' War for five thousand dollars.

Man o' War wasted little time in earning the "de mostest hoss" title. As a two-year-old in 1919, racing in Riddle's black-and-gold silks, he went to the post ten times, winning nine races, and in six of those he carried 130 pounds, an unheard of challenge by today's standards. His sole defeat was in the Sanford Memorial Stakes at Saratoga, where he broke poorly, was trapped on the inside, and, when clear, couldn't catch the leader, the aptly named colt Upset. Man o' War carried 130 pounds; Upset, fifteen pounds less.

Riddle withheld Man o' War from the 1920 Kentucky Derby, feeling that a mile and a quarter race early in the season wasn't in his colt's best interests. Shortly, though, the fun began, with wins in the Preakness Stakes at Pimlico and the Belmont Stakes at Belmont Park, the track and the race named in honor of the father of Man o' War's breeder. Then it was on to the Stuyvesant Handicap at Jamaica Racetrack in New York, where the three-year-old carried 135 pounds, thirty-two more than the only other starter. In the Dwyer

Stakes at the nearby Aqueduct track, he crushed the much-ballyhooed colt John P. Grier. Many felt that "Big Red" broke Grier's heart, for the defeated colt was never the same.

Man o' War also won the Travers Stakes, the Lawrence Realization (by one hundred lengths), and the Jockey Club Gold Cup. In the fall of 1920, Man o' War won the Potomac Handicap at Havre de Grace racetrack in Maryland, carrying 138 pounds. He closed his career by whipping Sir Barton, the first horse in history to sweep the Triple Crown, in a match race in Canada, knocking six and two-fifths seconds off the track record for one and a quarter miles.

Man o' War retired with twenty wins in twenty-one races, and he owned five track records, ranging from a mile to a mile and five-eighths. At stud he sired American Flag and Crusader, winners of the Belmont Stakes in 1925 and 1926, respectively; Clyde Van Dusen, the 1929 Kentucky Derby winner; and War Admiral, his best son, the 1937 Triple Crown winner. Demonstrating his versatility as a sire, Man o' War sired Battleship and Blockade, winners of the world's most challenging steeplechase races, the English Grand National and the Maryland Hunt Cup, respectively, both in 1938. Battleship became an important sire of steeplechasers. Also, Man o' War's son Holystone was a champion show hunter.

A larger-than-life-sized statue of Man o' War by famous sculptor Herbert Haseltine greeted visitors to Riddle's Faraway Farm in Kentucky, where "Big Red" stood as a stallion, and where Will Harbut gave colorful descriptions of his horse's greatness. In October 1947, Harbut passed away, followed by Man o' War at age thirty a month later. Eventually, the statue was moved to the Kentucky Horse Park near Lexington.

Frank Voss' painting was done at Saratoga in the summer of 1919, when Man o' War was a two-year-old.

Man o' War

Collection of the National Museum of Racing and Hall of Fame, oil on canvas, 28 by 37 inches, 1919

Sir Barton is best remembered for being the first horse to sweep, in 1919, the three races that make up what is now known as the Triple Crown and for being defeated by Man o' War in a match race in Canada the following year.

A well-made chestnut with a large, irregular blaze, Sir Barton was foaled at John E. Madden's Hamburg Place in Kentucky. His sire, Star Shoot, a crack two-year-old in England, stood at stud at Hamburg Place and became America's leading sire five times in the second decade of the 1900s.

Early in his two-year-old year, Sir Barton raced in Madden's colors but shortly thereafter caught the eye of H. Guy Bedwell, a veteran horseman in Maryland who had just become the private trainer for Commander J.K.L. Ross, a newcomer to racing from Canada. Bedwell, nicknamed "Hard Guy," was a master of patching up cheap claiming horses and returning them to winning form. On the other hand, Ross, who served as a commander for the Royal Canadian Navy in World War I, aspired to own major stakes winners, and money was no object.

The Bedwell/Ross team didn't get off to a rousing start with Sir Barton, who cost $10,000, a sizable sum in that day. He failed to break his maiden in six starts at two. With shelly feet, Sir Barton was a difficult horse to train, and he had a nasty disposition.

Bedwell also purchased for Ross the small, nondescript gelding Billy Kelly, named for a sportswriter in Buffalo, New York. Billy wasn't much to look at, but he was a runner and became the champion juvenile male in 1918.

The entry of Billy Kelly and Sir Barton was favored in the Kentucky Derby, solely on Billy's accomplishments. The strategy was for Sir Barton to set a fast pace and for Billy Kelly to take over in the stretch. No dice. Sir Barton loved the heavy going and led the entire way, leaving his stablemate five lengths back at the wire. This was the first time a maiden had won the Derby, and the first time an entry had placed one-two.

That year's Preakness was held the Wednesday after the Derby. Four days of rest and a rail journey to Baltimore didn't deter Sir Barton. Again he led the entire way in what then was a mile and one-eighth race and went on to New York to win the Withers and Belmont stakes. He set an American record of 2:17 2/5 in the Belmont, which then was run at a mile and three-eighths.

In Maryland that fall, Bedwell saddled Sir Barton to win two handicaps, and the horse carried in excess of 130 pounds in each. At Saratoga the following summer Sir Barton was brilliant, winning in record times in two stakes, again carrying high weights.

By then, horse racing fans were clamoring for a match race between Man o' War and Sir Barton. After much haggling, the Kenilworth track at Windsor, Ontario, was chosen. Man o' War won by seven lengths over a cement-like surface, which the hometown fans felt was not to their horse's liking.

Sir Barton was a failure at stud, ending up at a U.S. Army Remount station in Wyoming, where he eventually stood for a stud fee of ten dollars. Sir Barton died in 1937 at age twenty-one. Commander Ross commissioned Sir Barton's portrait in happier days, when Sir Barton was a three-year-old at the height of his career.

Sir Barton

Collection of the National Museum of Racing and Hall of Fame, oil on canvas, 34 by 43 inches, 1919

Edward B. McLean of Washington, D.C., purchased The Porter as a three-year-old in 1918 after the son of Sweep had shown great promise the previous year with three wins in six starts. The Porter proceeded to win twenty-three races for McLean, including stakes races at ages three through six.

Upon retirement, The Porter stood in Leesburg, Virginia, at McLean's Belmont Plantation, which to this day is the site of popular steeplechase meets. The unbeaten Colin also stood at Belmont.

Using mostly homebreds, McLean was fifth on the list of winning owners in America in 1927. The following year he was the leading owner, with Toro, a son of The Porter, and Jock, by Colin, among the nation's top three-year-olds.

McLean, the one-time publisher of *The Washington Post*, also gained notoriety in Washington's social circles. In 1912 his wife, Evalyn Walsh McLean, bought in Paris a 45.52-carat diamond that had become known as

The Porter

Collection of Mr. & Mrs. C. Martin
Wood III, oil on canvas,
26 by 30 inches, 1920

the Hope Diamond, the ownership of which traces to King Louis XIV in 1668. Mrs. McLean was the first American owner. Following Mrs. McLean's death, the Hope Diamond was donated to the Smithsonian, where it is on permanent display. Despite his wealth and successes on the Turf, McLean led a tragic life. In 1933, after a court in Maryland held him to be mentally incompetent, McLean entered a sanitarium near Baltimore, where he died in 1941.

On the other hand, The Porter fared well. Upon McLean's retirement from racing in 1931, John Hay Whitney purchased The Porter for $27,000 to stand at his farm in Kentucky. The Porter's get included Foxcatcher Farm's Rosemont, winner of the 1937 Santa Anita Handicap by a nose over Seabiscuit. In 1937 The Porter was America's leading stallion.

The stables at the Oklahoma Training Track at Saratoga make a splendid background for Voss' painting, which was commissioned by McLean.

William Woodward bred Peanuts, a foal of 1922 with international bloodlines, his sire being the English stallion Ambassador IV, his dam the French mare Agnes Sard. But Peanuts, as suggested by his name, was tiny, which prompted his consignment to the Saratoga yearling sale. There, Robert L. Gerry purchased him for $2,100.

At two the little fellow, just a shade taller than fifteen hands, started sixteen times and won three minor races. However, Peanuts won four stakes as a three-year-old, becoming a big favorite with racing fans, who nicknamed him "Little Peanuts." At four he won the Edgemere Handicap after fighting side by side the length of the stretch with the good horse Pompey. Peanuts was durable, too, retiring in 1927 with eighteen wins in fifty-two starts.

My favorite Turf writer, John Hervey, described Peanuts in *Racing in America, 1922–1936*:

He deservedly ranks among the most interesting horses of recent times. A bay with the off pastern white, he was almost a perfect model within his miniature proportions. His head was fine and expressive, his neck of good length and, for a small horse, he stood over a lot of ground ... At the barrier, he was sometimes riotous. He did not always get away well, and it was in the stretch that he shone, the courage with which he would stand a long, hard drive being unqualified. It alone pulled him through in race after race.

Peanuts stood at stud at Gerry's Aknusti Stud, near Delhi, New York. Mares did not beat a path to his door, but, as Hervey wrote, "He begot in Top Row a son quite as remarkable as himself." Mrs. W. Plunket Stewart, well known in foxhunting circles, bred Top Row at her farm in Virginia. Top Row's dam, Too High — by name, a strange mate for Peanuts — won four races as a two-year-old but was winless in fifteen starts at three. Mrs. Stewart bred Too High to Peanuts largely because owner Gerry was her brother-in-law.

Peanuts

Collection of the National Museum of Racing and Hall of Fame, oil on canvas, 34 by 42 inches, 1926

Top Row, who was several inches taller than Peanuts, was a slow learner at two, but he finally broke his maiden as a three-year-old, then commenced racing in claiming races. Owner/trainer A.A. Baroni claimed him out of a race at Narragansett Park in Rhode Island for $3,500. In December 1934 Top Row went to California, where he suddenly came to life, winning a stakes race in world-record time. This prompted Baroni to enter Top Row in the first running of the Santa Anita Handicap, America's initial $100,000 race. Top Row got off poorly but made up ground to finish fourth in the twenty-horse field. Top Row returned east with a stop in Chicago, where he won a stakes race. Next on the agenda was a return to Narragansett Park, where he beat Alfred G. Vanderbilt Jr.'s Discovery, who at the time had won eight consecutive stakes races. In fairness, Discovery carried 139 pounds, twenty-nine pounds more than Top Row. In a rematch at Suffolk Downs in Massachusetts, Top Row again had Discovery's number, taking more than two seconds off a track record previously held by Discovery. By this time, Top Row was the talk of the Turf world and had earned the nickname "King of the Cast-Offs."

Back in California, Top Row set a track record at Santa Anita of 1:35 4/5 for the mile in a prep race for the 1936 Santa Anita Handicap. In a roughly contested stretch drive in the Big 'Cap itself, Top Row was the narrow winner, with his rival Discovery out of the money. His final race was at Tanforan in northern California, where he badly bowed a tendon and pulled up on three legs. Top Row retired with fourteen wins in forty-two starts and earnings of $213,870, a serious amount at the time.

Peanuts could justifiably be proud of his son. Likewise, he should have taken pride in Voss' portrait, which Nancy W. Gerry donated to the National Museum of Racing and Hall of Fame in 2001.

Foaled in 1925, Petee-Wrack was a product of William Woodward's breeding program, which was designed to produce winners of distance races like the mile and a half Belmont Stakes and England's two and a half-mile Ascot Gold Cup. Woodward imported Petee-Wrack's sire, Wrack, from England. Wrack sired the filly Flambino, whose son Omaha won the 1935 Triple Crown for Woodward. Omaha went to England in 1936 to be the sole Triple Crown winner yet to race in Europe. There he won several races and was beaten a nose in the Ascot Gold Cup. Flambino also produced Flares, who won the 1938 Ascot Gold Cup in Woodward's colors.

Petee-Wrack's female line is equally exciting. His dam, Marguerite, produced Gallant Fox, the 1930 Triple Crown winner for Woodward; Fighting Fox, the 1938 Wood Memorial winner; and Foxbrough, the 1938 champion juvenile in England. Gallant Fox was the sire of Omaha.

Woodward sold Petee-Wrack, who was Marguerite's first foal, as a yearling at Saratoga. The purchaser, John R. Macomber, was best known in steeplechase circles as the host of one of America's finest steeplechase meets. Macomber's Raceland meets were held in the 1920s through the mid-1930s at his estate in Framingham, Massachusetts.

Petee-Wrack was a hard-luck two-year-old, with no wins and four seconds. Two of his near misses, the Belmont and Pimlico

Petee-Wrack

Collection of the National Museum of Racing and Hall of Fame, oil on canvas, 32 by 40 inches, 1928

futurities, were roughly run, with Petee-Wrack the victim of fouls in the stretch in both. At three he won the Travers Stakes, in which champion Reigh Count suffered his sole defeat of the year. Petee-Wrack was brilliant in his four-year-old year, with four stakes wins, including the Metropolitan Handicap, and at five his wins included the Suburban Handicap.

Petee-Wrack stood as a stallion at Ellerslie Stud in Charlottesville, Virginia. His daughter, Columbiana, won the 1937 Widener Handicap at Hialeah, running the one and a quarter-mile distance in 2:01 4/5, which was reported to be the fastest time in history at that distance for a filly or mare. Steeplechase buffs hail Petee-Wrack as the sire of the winners of the four-mile Maryland Hunt Cup, the supreme test of a steeplechase horse, in four of five years. His son Peterski won in 1948; his Pine Pep, in 1949, 1950, and 1952. Hall of Fame member D.M. (Mikey) Smithwick rode both horses.

John Hervey described Petee-Wrack in *Racing in America, 1922–1936*:

A rich bay with black points, of size and substance, he stands over a lot of ground and has an exquisitely beautiful head.

Voss painted Petee-Wrack on the backstretch at Saratoga racecourse, the site of the Travers Stakes. John R. Macomber donated the painting to the National Museum of Racing and Hall of Fame in 1971.

Frank Voss painted George D. Widener's Jack High in the paddock at Belmont Park. This site is fitting, for it was at Belmont in 1930 that Jack High ran his most important race, winning the Metropolitan Handicap in 1:35, the fastest time to that date for the mile in the United States.

Jack High was one of 110 stakes winners bred by Widener from 1910 through 1971 at either his home farm, historic Erdenheim near Philadelphia, or at Old Kenney, his farm in Kentucky. Long before Widener's time, Erdenheim gained fame as the home of Leamington, who sired Aristides, winner of the first Kentucky Derby in 1875. Erdenheim was also the birthplace of Iroquois, who in 1881 became the first American-bred Epsom Derby winner.

Jack High's sire was John P. Grier. As noted in the piece on Man o' War, some thought John P. Grier's heart was broken when Big Red whipped him in the 1920 Dwyer Stakes. This theory can be disputed, as John P. Grier returned to win good stakes races, and he also became a creditable sire.

In 1928 at Saratoga, Jack High was a precocious two-year-old, upsetting Blue Larkspur and fourteen others in the Hopeful Stakes, and winning two other stakes. He raced through age six, with a career record of fifteen wins in thirty-four starts. At stud his best son was

Jack High

Private collection, oil on canvas,
28 by 36 inches, 1930

Lucky Draw, a gelding who won four stakes as a two-year-old and nine more stakes through age five. Like others owned by Widener, Lucky Draw did not contest the Kentucky Derby, as Widener felt that racing a mile and a quarter early in the season was detrimental to a horse's well being. On the other hand, Widener was an enthusiast for the mile and a half Belmont Stakes later in the spring. However, Lucky Draw could not run in the Belmont, as in his day geldings were not eligible. Widener had to wait until 1962, when Jaipur became the first to carry his distinctive dark blue-and-light blue silks to victory in his favorite race.

Jack High was also the sire of High Fleet, the champion three-year-old filly for Widener in 1936, and Lets Dine, the dam of Platter, Widener's champion two-year-old colt in 1943.

In addition to being a leading owner and breeder, Widener was a giant in the administration of racing. In 1950 he succeeded William Woodward as chairman of The Jockey Club, and in 1971 the National Museum of Racing named him its first Exemplar of Racing. Widener died in December 1971 at age eighty-two. The large animal hospital at the New Bolton Veterinary Center of the University of Pennsylvania bears his name. Erdenheim, too, continues to be prominent in American racing. It is now the stable name for horses campaigned by George Widener's nephew, F. Eugene Dixon, who lives at Erdenheim.

Equipoise, C.V. Whitney's dark chestnut colt, more than lived up to his nickname, "The Chocolate Soldier." Racing for six seasons commencing in 1930, he was an extremely willing soldier despite being plagued throughout by chronic quarter cracks. He started in fifty-one races, winning twenty-nine, and he was second or third in fourteen others. He was the champion two-year-old colt in 1930 with eight wins in sixteen starts, besting Twenty Grand, who went on to win the Kentucky Derby the following year.

Injuries precluded Equipoise from competing in either the Kentucky Derby or Belmont Stakes, though he finished fourth in the Preakness. He returned to form as a four-year-old and was Horse of the Year two straight years and top handicap horse three times. Perhaps his highlight was setting a world record of 1:34 2/5 at Arlington Park for the mile, under 128 pounds, while defeating the fine horse Jamestown, who carried ten pounds less. Equipoise also won the Suburban Handicap under 132 pounds and the Arlington Handicap with 135 pounds. His career earnings, $338,610, placed him second at the time to world leader Sun Beau. At stud he sired Shut Out, the 1942 Kentucky Derby winner. "The Chocolate Soldier" is a member of the Racing Hall of Fame.

John Hervey wrote in *Racing in America, 1922–1936*:

Equipoise's exact position among the great Thoroughbreds of America

Equipoise

Collection of Marylou Whitney,
oil on canvas, 42 by 48 inches, 1933

may be argued, but of one thing, however, there is no doubt. No horse that has appeared upon the turf in this present century, if ever, has been so ardently admired and even passionately loved by the great body of racing enthusiasts. That feeling extends also into the ranks of ordinarily cool and unimpassioned turfmen. The mere announcement that Equipoise was to appear was sufficient to draw a capacity crowd to any course in the country. This was at a time when on ordinary days the Great Depression had reduced the attendance to a corporal's guard.

Hervey likewise gave an eloquent description of Equipoise's physical characteristics:

A shade under 16 hands, he is a dark, liver-colored chestnut of a particularly rich and lustrous shade, here and there slightly but beautifully dappled, glinting with gold or deepening almost to a burnt tone. Without doubt, part of his charm for the public was his beauty, which was almost faultless, and the gay and gallant air displayed on his triumphs … His head was rather small, of fine almost delicate outline and great expressiveness, to which his eyes gave elegance. In bodily structure he was smooth, clean, closely knit and without overemphasis or development in any part.

Frank Voss has captured these characteristics in his painting of Equipoise during a morning training session at Saratoga. The painting of Equipoise was on loan to the National Museum of Racing for fifty years. However, in 2004, Whitney's widow, Marylou, placed the painting of Equipoise in her personal collection.

In 1915 Colonel E.R. Bradley, the famed owner/breeder and proprietor of Bradley's, a popular gambling casino in Palm Beach, Florida, imported from England two mares that became the second dams on both sides of Blue Larkspur's pedigree. Padula produced Blue Larkspur's sire, Black Servant; Vaila produced Blue Larkspur's dam, Blossom Time. The combined cost of Padula and Vaila was nine hundred dollars.

As indicated above, Bradley used B as the first letter in the names of his horses. The Bs had four wins in the Kentucky Derby in the 1920s and 1930s: Behave Yourself, Bubbling Over, Burgoo King, and Brokers Tip. However, Blue Larkspur, whom Bradley described as his best homebred ever, finished fourth as the heavy favorite in the twenty-one-horse field of the 1929 Derby, reportedly costing his owner a $125,000 wager. But Blue Larkspur had a bona fide excuse. The trainer was ill, and the assistant failed to have Blue Larkspur shod with caulks, disregarding the condition of the track, which was a sea of mud.

Blue Larkspur then won the Belmont Stakes, also on a muddy track, this time, you can be sure, with caulks. In all, Bradley's

Blue Larkspur

Collection of the National Museum of Racing and Hall of Fame, oil on canvas, 18 by 22 inches, 1934

favorite horse won ten of sixteen starts and was second or third four times in a career that was prematurely terminated by tendon problems. Nevertheless, Blue Larkspur's career earnings of $272,070 placed him third at the time to Sun Beau on the list of American money winners.

At stud Blue Larkspur was best known as a broodmare sire, ranking among the top ten broodmare sires from 1944 through 1960. His outstanding daughters included the champion sprinter Myrtlewood, Blue Delight, Bloodroot, Bee Ann Mac, and Blue Grass.

Frank Voss painted Blue Larkspur in his paddock at Bradley's Idle Hour Farm (now Darby Dan) in Kentucky. The portrait mirrors the description of Blue Larkspur by John Hervey:

He was a deep, rich bay with black points, whole colored, not a tall horse, of extreme elegance, with a lovely head, fine neck, oblique shoulder, round but not deep barrel and good bone.

Edward S. Voss, the artist's brother, donated the painting to the National Museum of Racing and Hall of Fame in 1955, when the museum moved to its permanent home in Saratoga Springs, New York.

William Woodward Sr., the owner/breeder of Gallant Fox, served in the early 1900s in the American embassy in London, where he acquired a fondness for horse racing. He brought a few mares back to America and commenced raising horses at Belair Stud, a farm near Bowie, Maryland, that had been formerly owned by Governor Samuel Ogle. The farm dated to pre-Revolutionary days but is now, sadly, the site of a huge housing development. However, history is preserved in the Selima Room at the public library in Bowie, which houses many of Woodward's books and memorabilia.

Woodward, in partnership with his close friend and adviser, Arthur B. Hancock of Claiborne Farm in Kentucky, imported from France the stallion Sir Gallahad III. Sir Gallahad III would sire Gallant Fox and become America's leading sire four times and leading broodmare sire a dozen times.

Woodward moved Gallant Fox as a weanling from Claiborne Farm to Belair Stud, and at two in 1929 the bay colt joined the stable of legendary trainer "Sunny Jim" Fitzsimmons. Early on Gallant Fox was immature and easily distracted, but he showed flashes of brilliance with two wins in seven starts in his juvenile year.

At three in 1930, Gallant Fox was awesome, right off, with victories in the Wood Memorial and the Preakness, which was run prior to the Kentucky Derby that year. The Preakness marked the first use at Pimlico of the starting gate, nicknamed at the time "the machine."

Lord Derby, whose ancestor lent his name to the title of the first Epsom Derby in England in 1780, attended the Kentucky Derby in 1930. A special pagoda was built at Churchill Downs to shelter the distinguished guest, who witnessed a truly "gallant" race, with Gallant Fox winning over Gallant Knight. Gallant Fox then won the Belmont Stakes to join Sir Barton in sweeping what soon became known as the Triple Crown.

Gallant Fox won nine of ten starts as a three-year-old and retired completely sound at year's end with earnings of $328,165, a world record at the time. "Sunny Jim," the trainer of many champions through the years, rated his Bold Ruler as his best horse at one mile, Nashua a nod over Gallant Fox in races at one and a quarter miles, and Gallant Fox easily the best at one and a half miles and more.

Turf historian John Hervey, who had a special gift for describing the physical characteristics of horses, wrote in *Racing in America, 1922–1936*:

There was about Gallant Fox an air of intense, almost flaming, vitality and dynamic force.

At stud Gallant Fox's first crop included Omaha, who in 1935 won the Derby, Preakness, and Belmont for Woodward. This was the year that Charlie Hatton of the *Daily Racing Form* popularized the term Triple Crown for these three races. Thus, Omaha became the first Triple Crown winner, though Sir Barton and Gallant Fox were honored retroactively. Gallant Fox's second crop included Granville, who won the 1936 Belmont. After this brilliant start, however, Gallant Fox had only marginal success as a stallion.

Mrs. William Woodward Sr. donated Gallant Fox's portrait to the National Museum of Racing and Hall of Fame in 1956.

Gallant Fox

Collection of the National Museum of Racing and Hall of Fame, oil on canvas, 31 by 36 inches, 1934

What with Laura Hillenbrand's best-selling book, a public broadcasting documentary that aired in 2003, and a feature movie later the same year, it would be presumptuous to think that I can add in any way to the Seabiscuit saga. However, I can share some personal memories.

By 1938, at the ages of fourteen and twelve, my older brother, Garry, and I had become avid fans of horse racing. Our interest was motivated in no small way by our stepfather, Bryce Wing, who was president of the National Steeplechase & Hunt Association, a steward at racetracks in Maryland, and the owner of a small string of racehorses.

For that matter, Garry and I were interested in many sports, but at the time, baseball and football were the only big league sports, with professional basketball and hockey in their infancy and soccer a non-entity. Horse racing, on the other hand, was truly a big deal in America, and the top horses were national heroes.

To be quite frank, the Winants brothers were War Admiral junkies. Our scrapbooks were full of articles and pictures of War Admiral sweeping the Triple Crown races in 1937. A rag-tag horse from California licking our hero? No way.

Prior to their match race at Pimlico in 1938, we read articles in the local newspapers, which then, unlike now, gave great coverage of horse racing, and we studied articles in *The Blood-Horse* and *Turf and Sport Digest* magazines. We were particularly taken by our copies of the official souvenir program, a publication of the Maryland Jockey Club, forty-two pages, ten by thirteen inches in

Seabiscuit

Collection of the National Museum of
Racing and Hall of Fame, oil on canvas,
34 by 52 inches, 1937

size, with a four-color cover and lengthy bios of the combatants.

On match race day Garry and I were excused early from school to watch War Admiral win at our favorite track, which was near our school. But he didn't, and in time our souvenir programs were placed in boxes with other memorabilia, completely forgotten, replaced by more current possessions, such as school yearbooks and pictures and programs of athletic teams on which we played.

Sixty or so years later I chatted with Laura Hillenbrand while she was doing research for *Seabiscuit*. I mentioned that I had attended the great match race and had fond memories, notwithstanding the fact that the "wrong" horse won. I also mentioned the souvenir program. "They're scarce as hens' teeth," she said. "Recently on eBay, one brought $1,800."

This, of course, got my attention, resulting in a mad scramble through boxes of childhood things. There, I found my program, and I donated it to the National Sporting Library in Middleburg, Virginia. In turn, the program was loaned to the National Museum of Racing for its Seabiscuit exhibition in 2003.

I must admit that I now feel far more kindly toward Seabiscuit than I did on that November afternoon when he whipped my horse.

Leslie Fenton, who was married to Marcella Howard, the widow of Seabiscuit's owner Charles S. Howard, presented Voss' portrait of Seabiscuit to the National Museum of Racing and Hall of Fame in 1962. As with my match race program, the painting was featured in the museum's special Seabiscuit exhibition.

The majority of horsemen have a problem horse at one time or another. Some give up in disgust, and the horse passes to other hands; others try one approach after another, and, sometimes, the bulb suddenly comes on and the horse fulfills its potential. This was the case with Calumet Farm's Whirlaway, who was a rogue early on. Then, in the patient and skilled hands of trainer B.A. (Plain Ben) Jones, he became a champion.

A foal of 1938, Whirlaway was a medium-sized dark chestnut, classically proportioned, with white markings behind and a star above the eyes that developed into a thin line down the center of his face. His trademark, though, was a long, flowing tail, which earned him the nickname "Mr. Longtail."

Whirlaway's sire, Blenheim II, won England's Epsom Derby in 1930 and sired 1936 Derby winner Mahmoud. Whirlaway's dam, Dustwhirl, a half sister to the good stakes winner Brevity, produced Reaping Reward, a major stakes winner.

Understandably, expectations were high, but as a youngster Whirlaway displayed an erratic disposition. He was extremely headstrong and rank, particularly in the saddling enclosure, and he viewed the starting gate as his enemy. He usually broke poorly from the gate, bringing up the rear in races, and when finally in gear often insisted on bearing out through the stretch, finishing in the middle of the track. As a result, he became Jones' special project, with visits to the paddock in morning training hours and schooling sessions in the starting gate. Also, Jones frequently grazed his pupil on a lead shank, perhaps using the time to discuss with his problem child the need for reform.

No one questioned Whirlaway's speed and stamina as a two-year-old, but his eccentricities resulted in only seven wins in sixteen starts. However, his victories included the prestigious Hopeful Stakes at Saratoga and the Breeders' Futurity at Keeneland, victories that prompted Turf writers to name him the 1940 champion juvenile colt.

Whirlaway continued to be a problem child early in his three-year-old year, which prompted Jones to equip him with a one-eyed blinker. A cup covering Whirlaway's right eye helped correct his tendency to bolt toward the outer rail. In the Kentucky Derby, with Eddie Arcaro up, Whirlaway was eighth in the field of eleven around the clubhouse turn, then made up ground on the backside and charged past the pack on the turn for home. He won by eight lengths in 2:01 2/5, a track record for one and a quarter miles that stood for more than twenty years. He was the first of Calumet Farm's eight Derby winners.

Whirlaway swept the other Triple Crown races in similar fashion and concluded the year with thirteen wins in twenty starts. At four he was equally effective with twelve wins in twenty-two starts. He was named Horse of the Year both years. As a five-year-old, Whirlaway was off the board in the Equipoise Mile at Arlington Park, where he pulled up noticeably sore and didn't respond to treatment. Mr. Longtail retired with thirty-two wins in sixty starts and earnings of $561,161, the first horse to win in excess of $500,000. At stud Whirlaway had marginal success, with eighteen stakes winners, including Scattered, the 1948 Coaching Club American Oaks winner. Commencing in 1949, Whirlaway stood at Marcel Boussac's stud in France, where he died at age fifteen.

Sports columnist Arthur Daley wrote in *The New York Times*:

Whirlaway will live long in memory, mourned by trainer Ben Jones as if he were the closest of blood relatives. "Plain Ben" loved Whirlaway just as a father grows to love a problem child who almost drives him to distraction. That's virtually what "Mr. Longtail" did to Jones.

The portrait of Whirlaway, which is one of twenty-three paintings that Voss did for Calumet owner Warren Wright, hangs in the Calumet Trophy Room at the International Museum of the Horse at the Kentucky Horse Park in Lexington.

Whirlaway

Collection of the International
Museum of the Horse, oil on canvas,
18 by 24 inches, 1944

The Whitney name has been synonymous with the American Turf from the late 1800s through the present day. The patriarch, William C. Whitney, made a fortune in developing New York City's transit system. By the 1890s he had sufficient time to become deeply involved in racing and breeding. Upon his death in 1904, his son, Harry Payne Whitney, furthered his father's interests and eventually bred a record 191 stakes winners, including the great Equipoise. A second son, Payne, wasn't interested in racing early on, but his wife, Helen Hay Whitney, became a great supporter of the sport. Racing under the stable name Greentree, she was the first lady of the Turf.

Helen Hay Whitney — the daughter of John Hay, who was Lincoln's secretary, and later ambassador to England and the U.S. secretary of state — started in steeplechasing before switching to flat racing. At Greentree Stud in Kentucky, she bred seventy-nine stakes winners, including Twenty Grand, the 1931 Kentucky Derby winner.

Shut Out, a foal of 1939, was sired by the great Equipoise. The derivation of Shut Out's name is a delight to baseball fans. His dam was Goose Egg, a fine stakes winner for Mrs. Whitney. As baseball lovers fully realize, a series of "goose eggs" or zeros on the scoreboard equals a shut out.

John M. Gaver, who had played on the baseball team at Princeton University, became Greentree's private trainer in 1939. In 1941 Gaver had a pair of talented juvenile colts in Shut Out and Devil Diver. Shut Out won the Grand Union Hotel Stakes at Saratoga, with Devil Diver third. Devil Diver then won the Hopeful Stakes over Shut Out. It was a rough race from which Shut Out emerged with contusions on his legs. Returned to the races in the fall, he was ineffective in four starts.

That winter the Greentree string trained in Florida. Shut Out came north to win the Blue Grass Stakes at Keeneland, where Devil Diver received rave reviews for winning the Phoenix Handicap over

Whirlaway, the previous year's Kentucky Derby winner. This performance prompted stable jockey Eddie Arcaro to choose Devil Diver over Shut Out as his mount in the Derby. Wrong choice. Shut Out, ridden by Wayne Wright, galloped home by two and a quarter lengths over Alsab, with Devil Diver sixth.

Greentree didn't fare well in the Preakness, with Shut Out fifth and Devil Diver eighth, well behind the winner, Alsab. The Belmont, though, was a different story, with Shut Out, this time ridden by Arcaro, winning by two lengths over Alsab. Shut Out went on to win the Arlington Classic and the Travers Stakes. Edward L. Bowen points out in his book, *Legacies of the Turf*, that no other horse since Shut Out had won the Derby, Belmont, and Travers until Thunder Gulch in 1995, some fifty years later. At four, Shut Out was inconsistent, with five wins including the Wilson Stakes at Saratoga, in seventeen starts. However, Devil Diver picked up the slack to become the champion of the handicap division twice.

John Hervey described Shut Out in *American Race Horses of 1942*:

When at the height of his form, Shut Out was unquestionably among the best three-year-olds ever seen in this country. He had everything — pedigree, speed, intense gameness … He was a finished and flexible racing tool of the first class.

Shut Out, whose portrait was done in the winner's enclosure at Belmont Park with Arcaro standing at his head, became the sire of Evening Out, who was the 1953 two-year-old filly champion, and of the stakes-winning colts Hall of Fame, One Hitter, and Social Outcast.

Upon Helen Hay Whitney's death in 1944, Greentree's racing and breeding interests were taken over by her son, John Hay Whitney, and her daughter, Joan Whitney Payson, who owned the New York Mets baseball team. Brother and sister ably carried on their mother's legacy for many years.

Shut Out

Collection of James E. Entrikin,
oil on canvas, 18 by 24 inches, 1944

Jockey Eddie Arcaro said that riding Calumet Farm's Citation was like driving a Cadillac. "You can get that chunk of speed whenever you ask for it." Starting in 1947, Citation's "chunks of speed" resulted in thirty-two wins in forty-five starts, and he was out of the money only once. He won twenty-two stakes races at twelve tracks in seven states to become the world's first equine millionaire.

Calumet's owner — baking powder tycoon Warren Wright — purchased Citation's sire, Bull Lea, as a yearling for $14,000. Bull Lea, a son of top stallion Bull Dog, won the Blue Grass, the Widener, and several other stakes, and he became the foundation sire that established Calumet as America's top breeding and racing operation. Bull Lea sired four horses that gained Horse of the Year status — Twilight Tear, Armed, and Coaltown, in addition to Citation — and three Kentucky Derby winners — Citation, Hill Gail, and Iron Liege.

Trained by Ben Jones, Citation, a bay that stood a bit over sixteen hands, won eight of nine starts at two. His sole defeat was by a stablemate, Bewitch, in a race in which Calumet's juveniles finished one-two-three. As a three-year-old in 1948, Citation won nineteen of twenty starts, including a sweep of the Triple Crown races. That fall he won two major stakes races in an incredible four-day span — the Sysonby Mile on Wednesday and the two-mile Jockey Club Gold Cup on Saturday. However, Citation paid a high price for his arduous campaign. Osselets (bony growths) formed on a front ankle, which shelved him for his entire four-year-old year. Upon returning to racing at five and six, Citation showed signs of his former brilliance, but he did not have the great consistency of his younger years, as evidenced by five wins and eight seconds in sixteen starts in 1950 and 1951. His highlights in those years were a world-record 1:33 3/5 for a mile at Golden Gate Fields and a brave second to Noor in the one and three-quarters-mile San Juan Capistrano Stakes at Santa Anita, where he gave the winner thirteen pounds and was beaten a nose in record time. Citation retired from racing after a victory in the 1951 Hollywood Gold Cup pushed him over the one-million dollar mark.

H.A. (Jimmy) Jones, who succeeded his father as Calumet's trainer, stated in the book *Royal Blood*:

Citation shouldn't have been brought back [after his injury]. *That was a mistake we made. If we hadn't brought him back to the races, he would have been recognized for what he was, the greatest of all … He didn't have a fault. He could sprint, he could go two miles, he could go in the mud, and he could go on a hard track. He could do it all, and that's the mark of greatness.*

Citation placed third to Man o' War and Secretariat on the poll by *The Blood-Horse* for the best one-hundred American racehorses of the twentieth century. At stud, though, Citation did not replicate his brilliance on the track, although his twelve stakes winners included Fabius, the 1956 Preakness Stakes winner, and the filly Silver Spoon, who beat colts in the Santa Anita Derby. Citation died in 1970 at age twenty-five.

I feel it is unfortunate that the paintings Voss did for Calumet are conformation portraits. None include images of Warren Wright, or the "Jones Boys" (the nickname often given Ben and Jimmy), or Eddie Arcaro, who so much enjoyed Citation's "chunks" of speed.

Citation

Collection of the International
Museum of the Horse, oil on canvas,
18 by 24 inches, 1948

Greentree Stable's Capot, a foal of 1946, upheld Greentree's tradition of horses with creative names. His sire was Menow, whose major claim to fame was thrashing War Admiral in the 1938 Massachusetts Handicap. Capot was out of Greentree's stakes-winning mare Piquet, and she's the source of Capot's name. Turf writer Joe Palmer explained in *American Race Horses of 1948* that in piquet, a card game, a capot is the equivalent of a grand slam in bridge. Capot didn't have a grand slam in the Triple Crown races in 1949, but he was close with a good second in the Kentucky Derby and wins in the Preakness and Belmont.

A great writer and a stickler for detail, Palmer also explained the pronunciation of Capot. "It's 'cap-ot,' not 'cap-o,' as the French would have it." Be that as it may, Capot, after a slow start in his two-year-old year, picked up steam that fall with wins in the Champagne Stakes at Belmont, the Wakefield Stakes at Jamaica, and the Pimlico Futurity. Ted Atkinson, who was under contract to Greentree, was the jockey.

In the spring of the following year, Capot took up where he had left off with a win in the Chesapeake Stakes at the Havre de Grace track in Maryland, then had disappointing thirds in the Wood Memorial at Jamaica and the Derby Trial at Churchill Downs. In these races, trainer John Gaver instructed Atkinson to rate Capot well off the pace, feeling this tactic would pay dividends in the mile and a quarter Kentucky Derby. Palmer quoted Atkinson on this strategy: "That colt just won't stand restraint. If I hold him back, he fights me, and then he hasn't any-

Capot

Collection of James E. Entrikin,
oil on canvas, 18 by 24 inches, 1950

thing left … There doesn't seem anything to do but let him run."

In the Derby there was no lying back for Capot, who was close to the front in the fourteen-horse field from the start. He challenged Olympia, the pacesetter (and favorite) after a mile, and put him away. Next, Palestinian challenged, and Capot signaled kaput for this fellow, too. The Greentree colt, however, couldn't withstand the stretch run by Calumet Farm's Ponder.

The Preakness was much of the same, but this time Capot hung in there, beating Palestinian by a head in 1:56, a track record for the mile and three-sixteenths. Ditto in the mile and a half Belmont Stakes, where Capot set the pace under slow fractions and held on to withstand Ponder's late charge by a half-length.

In the fall Capot won the mile Jerome Handicap at Belmont under top weight of 126 pounds, but his highlight was the Sysonby Mile, where he faced Calumet's four-year-old Coaltown, who had posted world and track records during the year. The two were at it hammer and tong the entire way, with Capot the braver, winning by a length and a half. They were rematched in the Pimlico Special, a match race, but it was no contest. Capot put Coaltown away early and coasted home by twelve lengths.

Turf writers chose Capot over Ponder as the champion three-year-old colt, and the Greentree runner shared Horse of the Year honors with Coaltown. The following year, however, was disappointing. Plagued with soundness problems (splints), Capot could only manage to win one of three starts, the Wilson Stakes at Saratoga. At stud Capot was a failure.

Christopher T. Chenery was a successful businessman as the head of several natural gas companies. He was also no slouch as a horse breeder at his farm, The Meadow, near Doswell, Virginia, some seventy-five miles south of Washington, D.C. Like most people who breed to race, he had looked forward to producing top-quality horses. There was little cause for optimism, however, when Chenery bred his mare, Hildene, bought at a dispersal sale for $750, to Princequillo, an Irish-bred who was a fine distance racer but at the time an unknown as a stallion. It was a convenient and an inexpensive mating: Princequillo stood at Ellerslie Farm in nearby Charlottesville at a stud fee of $250. Nevertheless, Chenery hit the jackpot, the offspring being Hill Prince, a foal of 1947 who became a national champion at two, three, and four. Furthermore, Hildene produced additional stakes winners for Chenery, including First Landing, a champion two-year-old who was third in the 1959 Kentucky Derby.

Trained by J.H. (Casey) Hayes, Hill Prince won six of seven starts at two, providing Princequillo with his first of sixty-five stakes winners. For the year Hill Prince nosed out King Ranch's Middleground in voting by Turf writers as America's leading juvenile colt in 1949.

At the end of Hill Prince's two-year-old campaign, Chenery decided that the colt would return to The Meadow for a rest, then be placed in training for the 1950 Kentucky Derby. Turf writers suggested that Derby prospects train best in Florida or California.

A hands-on horseman, Chenery explained his decision to stay home in *American Race Horses of 1950*:

Hill Prince has been turned out for the past two months [as of late December 1949], has not had a blanket on him, takes all the exercise he wants in a six-acre field and apparently has not let down too much. He now is a bit over sixteen hands, is solidly made, and is the best-balanced colt I have ever owned. His manners are nice; I can walk out in the pasture, catch him and bring him in by his halter without a lead shank.

Hill Prince came out in April under regular jockey Eddie Arcaro, who is astride Hill Prince in Voss' painting, to win a division of the

Experimental Free Handicap at Jamaica and the Wood Memorial at Belmont Park. In the Derby, though, he had to be content with a second to old rival Middleground. Hill Prince turned the tables on Middleground in the Preakness, but the rubber match, the Belmont Stakes, went to Middleground, with Hill Prince out of the money for the first time.

Hayes freshened Hill Prince and brought him back in the summer to win the American Derby in Chicago. Back east in the fall, Hill Prince won the mile Jerome Handicap. In the two-mile Jockey Club Gold Cup he faced Noor, a California invader who had set several world marks in beating the great Citation. Chenery's colt was the easy winner, four lengths in front of Noor. This race impressed the voters for year-end honors in 1950; Hill Prince was

Hill Prince

Collection of Walter J. Lee,
oil on canvas, 25 by 30 inches, 1951

the champion over Middleground, whose only wins for the year in ten starts came in the Derby and Belmont. Hill Prince was also named Horse of the Year, a first for a Virginia-bred. He paid dearly for success, though; a stress fracture in a front leg sidelined him until the fall of the following year. However, Hill Prince returned with a vengeance, his six starts including a five-length victory in the New York Handicap and a close second to Counterpoint in the Jockey Club Gold Cup. Despite this abbreviated campaign, Hill Prince was named champion handicap horse for his fourth title in three years.

In the winter of 1952, Hill Prince was retired following a disappointing effort in the Santa Anita Handicap. At stud he is best remembered for siring the full sisters Levee and Bayou. Both won major stakes races and were marvelous producers. Levee was the dam of champion race mare Shuvee; Bayou was the granddam of 1979 Belmont Stakes winner Coastal and of Slew o' Gold, champion at ages three and four in 1983 and 1984.

The Meadow was the birthplace in 1970 of Secretariat, who profited from the ownership and management of Chenery's daughter, Penny, after the death of Chenery in early 1973. Alas, the construction of a huge amusement park next door to The Meadow put an end to the proud farm.

Chapter Four

Steeplechasing

Frank Voss went to England in 1926 to foxhunt with his friend the Duke of Beaufort. The timing was good as his visit coincided with Jack Horner's victory in the Grand National for owner Charles Schwartz, a New York broker who, like Voss, lived on Long Island. Voss' painting of Jack Horner has the Aintree racecourse at Liverpool, the site of the Grand National, as its background.

Schwartz, who was well known as a polo player, sought to emulate the success of fellow polo player Stephen (Laddie) Sanford, who was the first American to own a Grand National winner, his Sergeant Murphy having turned the trick in 1923. Both Sergeant Murphy and Jack Horner were based in England and were trained and ridden by Englishmen.

Schwartz purchased Jack Horner, who was seventh in the 1925 Grand National, for four thousand pounds several weeks before the 1926 race. The winning jockey was William Watkinson, a Tasmania native who rode races with success in Australia before going to England. In 1922 Watkinson had been a close second in the Grand National.

Jack Horner

Collection of Kristine L. Matlack, D.V.M.,
oil on canvas, 34 by 43 inches, 1926

Reg Green described the highs and lows of Jack Horner's victory in *The History of the Grand National: A Race Apart*:

One of the few not to see the finish was Jack Leader, the trainer of the winner, who was slapped so hard by Charlie Schwartz that he fell off his perch in the stand … Schwartz wanted to give Watkinson a present of 4,000 pounds, but it was decided to give him 1,000 pounds a year for four years. Three weeks later, poor Watkinson was killed in a fall at Bogside, Scotland.

Kristine Matlack, an equine practitioner in Wisconsin who acquired the painting of Jack Horner from the Schwartz family, is quite a sportswoman in her own right. As the owner and trainer of Whackerjack, Matlack chose Olympic show-jumping rider Kathy Kusner to ride her horse in the 1971 Maryland Hunt Cup. This was the first time a female had ridden in the race, which dates from 1894. Kusner's presence caused considerable excitement and controversy, to put it mildly. Whackerjack finished fifth in the field of twelve, but, most importantly, Kusner's breakthrough paved the way for future successes by females in the Maryland Hunt Cup, a race that steeplechase fans compare in difficulty with the Grand National.

I debated whether to place the painting of Billy Barton and owner Howard Bruce in the foxhunting or the horse racing sections of this book and chose the latter because Billy Barton gained fame in steeplechase racing. That is not to say that Billy Barton wasn't a crack field hunter; he gave Bruce, master of the Elkridge Hounds in Maryland in the 1920s, countless days in the hunting field.

Billy Barton showed signs of brilliance in flat racing, his wins including the Cuban Derby in Havana. He mostly attracted attention, however, because of his unruly disposition. On one occasion, half a dozen men were needed to force him to leave the paddock for a race at Pimlico, and he often waged mighty battles to avoid being placed at the starting barrier. In time, he was ruled off the flat tracks, and Howard Bruce was able to purchase him for a song as a hunter prospect.

First, Bruce had his new horse gelded, and, when the time came, Billy Barton immediately took to jumping fences. From the outset, though, he had an unusual style, holding his head high over fences and kicking back with his rear feet at the top of his arc. In the 1924 and 1925 foxhunting seasons, Billy Barton went out eighty-one times. With those hunts under his belt, Billy Barton was next turned to racing over timber fences, a sporting highlight in Maryland each spring.

Albert G. Ober, an honorary whipper-in for the Elkridge Hounds and Bruce's close friend, rode Billy Barton in 1926 to win the Grand National Point-to-Point in their first start. The next week they followed that win with a victory in the Maryland Hunt Cup, the most challenging timber race in the United States. The following Saturday, Billy Barton won Virginia's most prestigious timber race, the Virginia Gold Cup. The feat of winning the Hunt Cup and the Gold Cup in the same year has never been duplicated. Billy Barton fell in the Hunt Cup in 1927, but he won three major races that autumn for a record of seven wins in eight starts.

In November 1927, Billy Barton went to trainer Aubrey Hastings in England to prepare for the 1928 English Grand National. Bruce wanted Ober to ride, but Hastings felt strongly that an English professional jockey was preferable. He chose Tom Cullinan.

Burgoright, also a Maryland Hunt Cup winner, joined Billy Barton in the field of forty-two starters. His rider was Frank A. (Downey) Bonsal, a top amateur from Maryland. Easter Hero, a veteran chaser who was one of the favorites, played a key role in the outcome of the race through an unfortunate incident at Canal Turn, the seventh of thirty fences in the four and a half-mile race. He landed squarely on top of the fence, straddled it, and was stuck there for agonizing minutes while the majority of the field bore down on him. With horses refusing and taking evasive action, the ensuing pile-up was one of the worst in the history of the race, which dates from 1839. Burgoright was one of the unfortunates. Billy Barton, on the other hand, cleared the fence *and* Easter Hero with an incredible leap to be one of the few to make it through the melee. Billy Barton led for the next two and a half miles, jumping brilliantly, but his luck ran out at the last fence. Jumping alongside Tipperary Tim, he blundered and fell. Tipperary Tim, a 100-1 shot, went on to win, while Cullinan remounted Billy Barton to finish second. Billy Barton remained in England to try again in 1929, but he fell, ironically, at Canal Turn. Upon returning home, he went back to the hunting field.

Billy Barton

Collection of H. Bruce Fenwick,
oil on canvas, 28 by 46 inches, 1927

Billy Barton's death at age thirty-two in 1950 was described by Bruce in an article in *The Maryland Horse* magazine: "Billy Barton wasn't a friendly horse. I'd be in his stall and he'd come after me, ears back and teeth bared. One evening, he was relaxed and friendly. He nuzzled my chest, simply wasn't his old self. The next day, he was dead."

Billy Barton had connections, of a sort, with success in future Grand Nationals. Marion du Pont Scott's Battleship, a son of Man o' War, used a win in the Billy Barton Steeplechase at Pimlico as a stepping stone to victory in the 1938 English Grand National. Howard Bruce's grandson, Charles C. Fenwick Jr., rode Ben Nevis II to win the 1980 Grand National. Another of Bruce's grandchildren, H. Bruce Fenwick, a successful rider in timber races for many years, owns Frank Voss' lovely painting of Billy Barton in the hunt field.

Maude K. Stevenson's Alligator won his share of America's top timber races in the late 1920s and early 1930s, including the Meadow Brook Cup on Long Island, the New Jersey Hunt Cup, and the Rose Tree Challenge Cup in Pennsylvania. He is best remembered, however, for the 1929 Maryland Hunt Cup and the 1930 International Gold Cup at the Grasslands course in Tennessee. In both races Alligator fell, and his rider, Charlie Plumb, father of international three-day-event rider Mike Plumb, remounted to finish first.

Talented race rider William B. Streett covered the 1929 Maryland Hunt Cup for *The Sportsman* magazine. He noted that fourteen horses went to the post in the four-mile, twenty-two-fence race, and that Alligator fell at the second fence. Riding Reelfoot in the race, Streett set the pace. He wrote:

It was going into the fifteenth fence that I finally located Alligator. He was coming like a cannon ball, but I had a big advantage over him — it must have been three or four hundred lengths — and Reelfoot was running very strongly and fencing well. By the nineteenth fence, though, Alligator, incredibly, was only three lengths back. Reelfoot hung on gamely as he could, but Alligator was too quick. He rolled into the last fence with a two-length advantage and won by just about that margin.

The International Gold Cup was America's version of the English Grand National, and to give it more appeal His Majesty Alfonso XIII, the king of Spain and an enthusiast of horse sports, provided a gold challenge cup. Writing in *The Sportsman*, "Huntsman" described the construction of the twenty-six brush fences on the four and a half-mile Grasslands course:

The obstacles were formidable enough for anyone. None were over five feet high, and they didn't have drops on the landing side. However, they were so solid and thick that liberties could not be taken. A horse had to jump high, wide and handsome to be safe, and do that 26 times to finish. On the whole, the course struck me as not quite as severe as Aintree [the site of the English Grand National], but by long odds the second most difficult that I have ever seen, and much the most difficult brush course in this country.

"Huntsman" stated that the footing was deep from weeklong rains for the seventeen starters, including three from England. He wrote:

As the leaders came out of the mist and down the hill for the final time, we saw that there were only two horses remaining in the race, Alligator, ridden by Charlie Plumb, and Waverley Star, Jack Skinner up. They took four fences almost together. One more fence and then the stretch.

Alligator rose first, hit the fence and came down. Waverley Star landed safely, but turned to avoid falling over Alligator. In the process, he missed his footing, slipped and fell. There he lay, his wind knocked out. Alligator, on the other hand, was unhurt. Mr. Plumb remounted and rode him in, the winner.

The International Gold Cup was held again in 1931, with Richard K. Mellon's Glengesia the winner. The Grasslands meet then became the victim of the Great Depression. At the time, Mellon was the guiding force behind the Rolling Rock steeplechase meet in western Pennsylvania. Permission was granted to transfer the International Gold Cup, along with King Alfonso's gold cup, to Rolling Rock, where it was held through 1983, when Rolling Rock ceased operation. The International Gold Cup is now a feature each autumn over timber fences at the Great Meadow course in Virginia.

Frank Voss' portrait of Alligator was done at the Meadow Brook course on Long Island. The author inherited the painting upon the death of his stepfather, S. Bryce Wing, in 1975.

Alligator

Collection of Peter Winants,
oil on canvas, 28 by 36 inches, 1929

Frank Voss painted William du Pont Jr.'s Ruler at Belmont Park, where the son of Horron won the Brook Steeplechase Handicap in 1929 and 1930 to become the first of du Pont's thirty-four homebred stakes winners. Ruler was also second in the Saratoga Steeplechase Handicap in 1928 and 1929. George H. (Pete) Bostwick, shown wearing du Pont's distinctive silks of sapphire blue with a gold fox on front and back, was Ruler's jockey. A hands-on horseman, du Pont, with a rub rag hanging from his pocket, is holding Ruler.

Upon du Pont's death in 1966 at age sixty-nine, an obituary in *The Blood-Horse* described him as "a man who can run a bandage, exercise a horse, ride a race, breed a top-class runner and build a racetrack."

The obit could have added that du Pont also skillfully hunted a pack of foxhounds. In 1912, when still a schoolboy, he started a private hunt at his family's estate, Montpelier, in Virginia. His sister, Marion, who became legendary in steeplechase racing, accompanied him on hunts. In 1926 du Pont took his hounds to Fair Hill, Maryland, to hunt as the Foxcatcher Hounds. In recognition of his fifty-seven years in the sport, du Pont is enshrined in the Huntsmen's Room, the ultimate honor for foxhunters, at the Museum of Hounds and Hunting in Morven Park, Virginia.

Du Pont also rode races at hunt meetings up and down the East Coast, and he designed steeplechase courses. In 1934 he was the founder and course designer of the Fair Hill race meeting. Additionally, he rode the winner of a race at the inaugural meet.

Du Pont will be best remembered, however, for breeding stakes winners in flat racing. Among the best horses he bred and raced in the name of Foxcatcher Farm was Berlo, champion three-year-old filly in 1960. Other homebreds include Fairy Chant, champion three-year-old filly in 1940 and champion handicap mare in 1941, and Parlo, a three-time champion mare in the mid-1950s. His best colt was Rosemont, who won the 1937 Santa Anita Handicap, giving ten pounds to runner-up Seabiscuit. At the dispersal sale of du Pont's stock in 1966, Paul Mellon purchased the mare All Beautiful, who became the dam of Arts and Letters, second in the Kentucky Derby and Preakness and winner of the Belmont Stakes and the Travers Stakes in 1969.

The Blood-Horse concluded in du Pont's obituary:

Mr. du Pont's material and moral support of the sport of racing was great. His counsel was invaluable, for although he spoke seldom, and then quietly, he knew what he was talking about.

Ruler

Collection of Peter R. Coggins, M.D., oil on board, 24 by 32 inches, 1932

"RULER"

...OCK STEEPLECHASE 1929 AND 1930

...MONT PARK

...PERTY OF FOXCATCHER FARMS

FBVOSS

1932

reen Cheese won the 1931 American Grand National, in which he set a course record that stood for twenty-five years, and he also captured the 1932 Broadhollow Steeplechase Handicap. Mrs. John Hay (Liz) Whitney was the owner, and Rigan McKinney, the rider. (A reproduction of Voss' painting of Liz Whitney Tippett is on page 135.)

McKinney, a native of Ohio, had great success in his youth with show hunters, and at fourteen he won his first race, on the flat at a local country fair. He soon caught the attention of steeplechasing's foremost trainer, Thomas Hitchcock Sr., of Long Island and Aiken, South Carolina. Hitchcock encouraged and brought along many aspiring race riders, including George H. (Pete) Bostwick, who rode in the same era as McKinney. Riding as an amateur against the country's best professional jockeys, McKinney won stakes races for Hitchcock on such fine horses as Rioter, Chenango, Annibal, Amagansett, and Ossabaw. He often said, though, that Green Cheese was his favorite.

Green Cheese

Private collection, oil on canvas,
28 by 36 inches, 1933

McKinney led the national steeplechase lists in both races won and purses earned in 1933, 1936, and 1938. He retired with 147 wins, which remains a record for amateur steeplechase jockeys. At this writing, he stands fifteenth on the all-time list of American jump jockeys, both amateur and professional. With these accomplishments he was admitted to the Racing Hall of Fame. McKinney then turned to training steeplechase horses for his mother, Mrs. Corliss Sullivan, and oth-

ers. He scored repeat wins in many of the stakes he'd won as a jockey. McKinney stepped down as a trainer in 1953 to become a commercial breeder of Thoroughbreds at his Blarney Farm in Maryland. In 1963 he moved his business to Kentucky.

McKinney's children and stepchildren have inherited their father's love of sport. His daughter, Kathleen Crompton of Unionville, Pennsylvania, is a lifelong foxhunter and has owned horses in timber racing. She now has several Thoroughbred broodmares and breeds for the yearling sales. McKinney's stepdaughter, F. Lee McKinney, trains racehorses in Kentucky. She owns and trains Feeling So Pretty, the champion race mare over fences in America in 2003. Laura McKinney runs her stepfather's former farm in Kentucky with help from another stepdaughter, Ouisha, who markets her creative talents in knitting and ceramics. Daughters Tamara and Sheila gained fame as alpine ski racers. In 1983 Tamara became the first American woman to win the overall Alpine World Cup championship, and she competed in the Olympics in 1980, 1984, and 1988. Tamara now lives in California, where she has had success with show jumpers. Sheila is a helper on the family farm, and she has returned to riding show hunters after an absence of nearly twenty years.

Voss painted Green Cheese and McKinney, who died in 1985 at the age of seventy-seven, on the steeplechase course at Belmont Park, the site of their big wins.

John M. Schiff's Indigo — a son of Stefan the Great out of a mare by Rock Sand, who was also Man o' War's broodmare sire — wasn't quite fast enough to race successfully in steeplechases over brush fences. In four starts in 1934, he was either third or fourth. However, when switched in the fall of that year to races over timber fences, where jumping ability and endurance are more important than sheer speed, he had two wins in as many starts. Indigo's rider was Burley Cocks.

The 1935 season was a banner one for the big gray gelding. In nine starts, all over timber, Indigo won six races and had two seconds and a third. His wins included the Virginia Gold Cup, the Meadow Brook Cup, and the New Jersey Hunt Cup. He was named timber racing's Horse of the Year.

Indigo's Virginia Gold Cup was particularly noteworthy. According to *The History and Origins of the Virginia Gold Cup*, mowers had clipped the grass on the track between the fences. In walking the course prior to the race, Cocks noted that a flag on a turn had not been replaced after the mowing. Slyly, but completely aboveboard, Cocks guided Indigo on a shortcut through high grass on this turn, while the others stayed on the neatly mowed track. This saved ten or so lengths, more than enough for the win. The race, though, was one of the final ones for Cocks, who fractured his skull several weeks later in a fall at the Radnor meet in Pennsylvania. This resulted in Cocks' retirement as a jockey and paved the way for his hugely successful career as a steeplechase trainer. He is a member of the Racing Hall of Fame.

Indigo won the 1936 Carolina Cup in Camden, South Carolina, and he gave his all in the 1937 Maryland Hunt Cup. Ridden by Sidney Watters Jr., he jumped the last fence a length behind Welbourne Jake.

Indigo

Collection of Mr. & Mrs. Peter G. Schiff,
oil on canvas, 28 by 36 inches, 1935

He closed ground through the stretch but fell short by a half-length in America's most challenging steeplechase.

Indigo's owner, John M. Schiff, was an avid foxhunter with the Meadow Brook Hunt near his home on Long Island. In 1923 he rode in the Meadow Brook-Smithtown Hunt Point-to-Point, finishing behind the winner, who was ridden by Franklin Voss' brother, Edward S. (Ned) Voss. Burley Cocks, then a teenager, won the secondary race on the card.

After getting his feet wet as an owner of steeplechase horses, Schiff turned to flat racing, where his Northwood Stable's purple-and-white silks were carried to victory in important stakes races. His Droll Role won six stakes races, including the 1972 Washington, D.C., International. Plugged Nickle, whose misspelled name was due to a clerical blip, won the Florida Derby and the Wood Memorial in 1980 and was named champion sprinter. Oleg Dubassoff was Schiff's trainer for thirty years, followed briefly by Scotty Schulhofer, who formerly had ridden Schiff's steeplechase horses, then Tommy Kelly.

Schiff died in 1985. His son, Peter, has carried on his father's love of racing, and, like his father, races horses on the flat and over fences. Tommy Kelly's son, Pat, trains the Schiff flat horses; Tom Voss, the jumpers. Racing under the name Fox Ridge Stable, Peter's steeplechase stakes winners include Petroski, winner of the 1996 New York Turf Writers Handicap at Saratoga, and Anofferucantrefuse, winner of the 2003 A.P. Smithwick Memorial, also at Saratoga.

Voss painted Indigo at the Meadow Brook Cup racecourse. Trainer Charles Hicks holds Indigo.

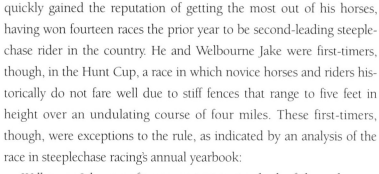

Welbourne Jake got Paul Mellon off on the fast track as a racehorse owner by winning the 1937 Maryland Hunt Cup, the most prestigious race over timber fences in the United States. This prompted the sportsman from Virginia to become seriously interested in steeplechasing. Mellon eventually switched to flat racing and became an international leader in breeding and racing. He had many marvelous horses throughout the years, but he will be best remembered as the owner and breeder of Mill Reef, winner of England's Epsom Derby and France's Prix de l'Arc de Triomphe in 1971, and Sea Hero, winner of the Kentucky Derby in 1993. Both were raised at Mellon's Rokeby Farm in Virginia.

One may well conclude that Welbourne Jake's name had a connection with Welbourne, an historic estate in Upperville, Virginia, that is in the hunting territory of the Piedmont Fox Hounds, for which Mellon was master. Not so. Welbourne Jake was bred in Ireland, out of the mare Welbourne.

Marion du Pont Scott — who bred and raced horses at Montpelier, her estate near Orange, Virginia — imported Welbourne Jake to this country as a yearling in 1931 and turned him over to her trainer, Noel Laing. Laing rode Mrs. Scott's Trouble Maker to win the 1932 Maryland Hunt Cup, and they finished the course in the English Grand National the following year. But Trouble Maker met an untimely end, falling in the 1935 Maryland Hunt Cup and breaking his neck. This prompted Mrs. Scott to stop racing her horses over timber; she sold Welbourne Jake to Mellon in the winter of 1936.

John T. (Jack) Skinner of Middleburg, Virginia, a highly respected horseman, became Welbourne Jake's trainer. In prep races for the 1937 Maryland Hunt Cup, Skinner rode Welbourne Jake to victories in the Deep Run Hunt Cup in Richmond and the Middleburg Hunt Cup. In a race later that same day at Middleburg, Skinner fell and broke his collarbone. As a consequence, Skinner chose seventeen-year-old Johnny Harrison, a freshman at Princeton University, to ride Welbourne Jake in the Maryland Hunt Cup. The Pennsylvanian had

quickly gained the reputation of getting the most out of his horses, having won fourteen races the prior year to be second-leading steeplechase rider in the country. He and Welbourne Jake were first-timers, though, in the Hunt Cup, a race in which novice horses and riders historically do not fare well due to stiff fences that range to five feet in height over an undulating course of four miles. These first-timers, though, were exceptions to the rule, as indicated by an analysis of the race in steeplechase racing's annual yearbook:

Welbourne Jake, very fit, was content to stay back of the early pace, moved up with the leaders in the last half-mile and drew slowly away to win without difficulty. He was perfectly ridden, and fenced beautifully, particularly over the larger fences.

In September 1937, Welbourne Jake slipped and fell while turned out in his paddock, breaking a leg. Just how great he would have been is anybody's guess. He'd won four of five starts over timber against top competitors. At age seven, young by timber racing standards, he appeared on the brink of a great career.

Johnny Harrison went on to become one of the best steeplechase riders of his era, winning ninety-nine races and more than holding his own against top professional jockeys at the hunt meetings and major tracks. But, as in the case of Welbourne Jake, tragedy struck: Harrison died from head injuries in a fall at Belmont Park in 1944.

Frank Voss painted Welbourne Jake, Jack Skinner up, at Glenwood Park, the site of their victory in the 1937 Middleburg Hunt Cup. Skinner often told friends that it's bad luck to have a portrait of a horse done prior to the retirement of the horse. So true, in this case.

Mellon gave the painting to Jack and Mildred Skinner. Skinner passed away in 1964; upon Mrs. Skinner's death in 2000 at age 103, the painting was left to her son, Howard Kaye. It hangs in the living room of Mr. and Mrs. Kaye's house, which, appropriately, borders the Glenwood Park course in Middleburg.

Welbourne Jake

Collection of Mr. & Mrs. Howard Kaye,
oil on canvas, 24 by 36 inches, 1937

Anderson Fowler of Far Hills, New Jersey, rode his horse, Peacock, to victory at various hunt meetings in the 1930s. In those days two types of steeplechase horses existed — those that ran for trophies at the country meets up and down the Eastern Seaboard and those that raced at the major racetracks such as Pimlico, Laurel, Belmont, Aqueduct, and Saratoga. The major tracks, which for the most part had a steeplechase each weekday from April through October, drew the best horses, which were usually ridden by professional jockeys. The country meets, on the other hand, featured amateur riders such as Andy Fowler on horses such as Peacock that in many cases were owned by their riders.

In 1934 Fowler rode Comea in the Maryland Hunt Cup, the most prestigious race on the hunt meeting circuit. Horse and jockey did not have an auspicious beginning. On the way to the start, they fell in a ditch. Reunited, they finished seventh. The 1935 season was Fowler's best. He had fourteen wins in fifty-four races to place fourth in a division of amateur riders that was heavily laden with talent.

During his undergraduate years at Princeton, Fowler rode races on weekends during the spring and fall. In a 1988 interview in *The Blood-Horse* magazine, the always-humble Fowler said, "I'm afraid that I didn't get much accomplished as a student because I was always involved in hunt meets and other sporting activities." However, Fowler did graduate, and he went on to considerable accomplishments.

Upon enlisting in the army at the outbreak of World War II, Fowler received his first assignment of instructing horsemanship at Fort Riley, Kansas. His pupils included the well-known jockey Basil James, big-time flat trainer Buddy Hirsch, and heavyweight-boxing champion Joe Louis. "If I had any trouble, I'd transfer the matter to Joe. He'd straighten it out," Fowler said. Later, Fowler saw action in

Peacock

Collection of Mr. & Mrs. E. Edward
Houghton, oil on canvas,
28 by 36 inches, 1939

the Pacific and participated in the landing at Leyte. He was awarded the Bronze Star.

Following the war, Fowler led a career that balanced sport, civic service, and the breeding and racing of Thoroughbreds. He was the master of the Essex Foxhounds in New Jersey, which was one of the finest hunts in America; president of the New Jersey Thoroughbred Breeders Association; board member and treasurer of Monmouth Park; and a member of The Jockey Club. He held a number of elective offices, including eight years in the New Jersey legislature as an assemblyman. "I ran for practically every office in Somerset County," Fowler said. "My only claim to fame in politics was that I never lost an election."

Fowler named one of his homebred stakes winners Assemblyman. Some of his other stakes winners over the years included Timely Warning, Baitman, Raritan Valley, Green Alligator, Master Speaker, and Master Dreamer. Fowler's daughter and son-in-law, Binnie and Eddie Houghton, own and operate Buckingham Farm in Maryland, where Fowler kept his broodmares.

Fowler attended the Kentucky Derby in 1969 when Majestic Prince narrowly defeated Paul Mellon's Arts and Letters. "We went there in style, aboard Mr. Mellon's private jet. We were back home in time for dinner," he said. Fowler returned to the Derby in 1991 with Green Alligator. This time he stayed for dinner and some celebrating: Green Alligator finished fourth.

Fowler's first wife, the former Genevieve Brady, died in 1965. She was the sister of James Cox Brady, the chairman of the New York Racing Association and vice chairman of The Jockey Club. Mrs. Fowler's nephew, Nicholas Brady, was president of The Jockey Club, and he served as secretary of the U.S. Treasury under presidents Ronald Reagan and George H.W. Bush.

Anderson Fowler died in 1997.

It is fitting that the steeplechase horses Genancoke (the gray) and American Way should share a Voss painting. Both were bred and raced through lengthy careers for Paul Mellon's Rokeby Stable, and they sometimes faced each other in stakes races.

In 1948 American Way, trained by John T. (Jack) Skinner, was steeplechasing's Horse of the Year and leading money winner. However, American Way was much indebted to Genancoke, who frequently served as a pacemaker, enabling American Way to come from off the pace for wins in important races, including the American Grand National. In the fall of 1948, Genancoke escaped American Way's shadow to win a major stakes race at Pimlico.

Mellon described the backgrounds of Genancoke and American Way in his autobiography, *Reflections in a Silver Spoon*:

Ivor Anthony [Mellon's trainer in England] *had sold me Makista, the mare on whom I had been second in the Bathurst and Oakdale point-to-point in England. I brought her back to the United States, but the firmer going didn't suit her feet. Just before the*

Genancoke and American Way

Collection of the National Museum of Racing and Hall of Fame, oil on canvas, 27 by 35 inches, 1950

war, I bred her to a stallion in Virginia called Gino. While I was out at Fort Riley [in Kansas on army duty] *she had a gray colt foal. In this manner, I was launched into the breeding world and into the problems of naming the progeny. Makista's foal acquired his name by a particularly circuitous route. Jimmy Brady's sister, Genevieve, was married to Andy Fowler, an amateur steeplechase jockey who was in our group at Fort Riley. Andy and Gen Fowler rented a house on the other side of the street from Mary and me. Gen Fowler liked drinking gin and Coke, so Makista's foal came to be called Genancoke. I also bought a mare called Sundance, and she foaled in the same year another colt by Gino, whom I named, more simply, American Way.*

In 1947 American Way became Mellon's first stakes winner as a breeder. This paved the way for many stakes wins by horses bred at Mellon's Rokeby Farm, near Upperville, Virginia, in some of the world's premier races.

Voss' painting, which Paul Mellon gave to the National Museum of Racing and Hall of Fame in 1999, shows Genancoke and American Way cooling out after a race at Belmont Park.

Chapter Five

Foxhunting

Frank Voss' picture of his father, William, one of the founders of the Rockaway Hunt Club on Long Island in 1878, was done in 1905, when the fledgling artist was twenty-five. Mr. Voss is depicted riding Wizard, a 16.3-hand Thoroughbred purchased from Robert North Elder Sr. of Maryland, who was the elder Voss' cousin. *The Chronicle of the Horse* used this art on its cover in 1954, a year after Frank's death. In the same issue of the *Chronicle* was an account of a day with the Rockaway Hunt from the September 5, 1880, issue of the *New York Post*:

The meet was held at the kennels near Lawrence Station yesterday afternoon. Punctually at 5 o'clock Mr. J. D. Cheever, the Master, appeared, followed by nine couples of hounds. It is noticeable that the hounds on this hunt, instead of being imported from England, were the well-known black-and-tan strain of Virginia and Maryland. These dogs differ from the English ones in that they are larger, faster and give more tongue on the scent.

The crowd of carriages and their occupants, scattered along the sloping hillside, made a pretty sight, but this did not last long, for in a few moments, the hounds proceeded to the covert, where a find was soon made. They then

William Voss

Collection of Thomas H. Voss,
gouache, 16 by 20 inches, 1905

struck a line of country to the westward, followed by the riders, among whom were Mr. Belmont Purdy, Master of the Meadow Brook Hunt, Mr. August Belmont, Jr., Miss Rogers of Washington, D. C., Mr. Alexander H. Stevens, Mr. Louis Neilson, Mr. Henry Munn of the Essex County Hunt, Mrs. Purdy, Mr. William Voss, Miss Dickerson, Mr. Edward Spencer and many others who did not follow the hunt as closely.

The hounds continued westward over a fair hunting country for three miles, and afforded an occasional view to those who followed in the carriages. At this point they made a sharp turn to the south, crossing the turnpike near Woodsburg Pavilion, where most of the field were well up to the hounds. Here it could be seen that the fences were in better condition, being much higher and stronger. After keeping up a rapid pace for two miles more, a short view-chase ensued, when the hounds soon overtook and killed the fox. The run was one of a little over seven miles and occupied about forty-five minutes.

Foxhunting ceased at Rockaway in the 1920s due to excessive urbanization. However, the Rockaway Club exists to this day. A Frank Voss painting of a steeplechase at Rockaway in bygone days hangs in the clubhouse.

J Watson Webb was the master of the Shelburne Hounds near Burlington, Vermont, for fifty years, from 1905 to 1955. He also was a key member of the Masters of Foxhounds Association, which was founded in 1907 as the governing body of the sport, and its president from 1948 to 1954.

Webb's son, Samuel B. Webb, described his renowned father in Alexander Mackay-Smith's book, *Masters of Foxhounds*:

Father was born in 1884, and he was never very far away from a horse or a hound, be it a coach horse, polo pony, quail pony, Scottish moor pony or Alaskan packhorse. In hunting, English and Welsh hounds were his preferences. He also bred a terrier for going to ground known as the Shelburne. These terriers went to almost every state in the union.

Webb started his Shelburne Hounds in 1903 as a beagle pack and switched to foxhounds in 1905. His pack was one of the first to be recognized by the Masters of Foxhounds Association. Shelburne hunted two or three days a week during September, October, and November over an open, rolling countryside with small coverts on the eastern shores of Lake Champlain, seventy-five miles or so from the Canadian border.

Samuel Webb reminisced:

All of Father's five children hunted, and in the early years a good many officers from nearby Fort Ethan Allen joined in. The majority of the field, though, usually consisted of family and friends. [The guest books in 1922, 1925, and 1951 list the presence of Frank Voss.] Due to Father's failing health, the hounds were disposed of in 1955 … In 1960, I was the master of

J. Watson Webb

Collection of Shelburne Museum,
oil on canvas, 28 by 26 inches, 1923

ceremonies at my parents' golden wedding anniversary. I think I enjoyed that occasion as much as they did. By the end of the year, they both passed away, but the heritage they left their children will always be priceless.

My wife and I visited the Shelburne Museum in the summer of 2003. I don't want to sound like a travel agent, but you are missing the boat if you haven't gone there. The museum, created in 1937 through the efforts of Mrs. Webb, has fine collections of folk art, decorative arts, and paintings by Monet, Cassatt, Degas, Andrew Wyeth, Grandma Moses, and a guy named Voss. Children (and this adult, too) enjoy boarding the refurbished steamboat, *Ticonderoga*.

And don't miss stopping by Shelburne Farms, several miles west of the museum, right on Lake Champlain. It's a fourteen-hundred-acre, nonprofit environmental research and education center. Many visitors come to study environmental issues; others, to walk the trails and visit the working dairy, the cheese-making facility, and the children's farmyard. Shelburne House, built in 1887 by Watson Webb's parents, is now a first-class inn. The view from the inn's lawns and gardens across Lake Champlain to the Adirondack Mountains in New York is a sight to behold.

End of the travel spiel. I departed fully appreciating that the area is a wonderland and that Frank Voss succeeded in capturing it at the time with his painting of J. Watson Webb on his favorite hunter, Vulture, and with five of his hounds. The names of the hounds and horse are found at the base of the painting.

SINBAD   GRAFTON   TALISMAN   VALIENT   VULTURE   PRIESTESS

Voss painted the late Frances Goodwin (married name Balding) of Beverly, Massachusetts, on Landboy, who was a crack steeplechase horse in the 1930s, when the sport was extremely popular in New England. Goodwin's daughter, Bettina Balding Blackford, said the hot-blooded Thoroughbred had the reputation of being a real challenge to the best male riders. "However, as soon as a sidesaddle was positioned on his back, he became an angel. My mother could go anywhere with him, do anything," Blackford said.

Frances Goodwin's father, Algernon Goodwin, was the master of the Myopia Hunt, one of the oldest and proudest in America. The hunt traces to a group of men who met to participate in sports such as baseball and tennis. Many of these men wore glasses, hence the name Myopia. The eyeglass wearers branched out into foxhunting, founding their hunt in 1882. To this day the followers of the Myopia Hunt enjoy drag hunting in their hunting country near Hamilton, Massachusetts. In drag hunting, hounds do not hunt the line of a fox; rather they follow a line made by dragging a bag soaked in fox scent or something similar.

The Goodwins wintered in Aiken, South Carolina, an area that is equally proud of its equine heritage. Thomas Hitchcock, the father of the famous polo player, stepped down as master of the Meadow Brook Hunt on Long Island in 1892 to establish his private pack of hounds in Aiken. The key hunting ground, an eight thousand-acre tract, became known as the Hitchcock Woods. Drag hunting over lines that wound through the woods became the vogue. The followers of the Aiken Hounds still gallop full tilt behind hounds through the Hitchcock Woods, leaping very jumpable post-and-rail fences laced with brush, known as Aiken fences.

This fine painting combines Voss' best talents. He has captured the feel of the lovely Hitchcock Woods and has attractively portrayed Frances Goodwin in her informal ("rat-catcher") attire, plus the likeness of the horse reflects the artist's high standards. The painting was a highlight of a Voss exhibition at the Morven Park Museum of Hounds and Hunting, near Leesburg, Virginia, in 1999.

Frances Goodwin

Collection of Bettina Balding Blackford,
oil on canvas, 24 by 36 inches, 1930

"Have hounds, will travel" would have been an appropriate motto for A. Henry (Alex) Higginson's Middlesex Hounds, which were headquartered in South Lincoln, Massachusetts, from 1901 through 1919. Higginson explained in his book, *The Hunts of the United States and Canada*, that his home territory was difficult to hunt because of dense woods and the abundance of wire. This prompted him to travel afar for sport.

In 1905 he took his hounds to Virginia to partake in the Great Foxhound Match and stayed the following year to hunt the nearby territory of the Loudoun Hunt. In 1907 Higginson's pack hunted the Millbrook Hunt's territory in Duchess County, New York, for the first of many visits at the invitation of Millbrook's master. In subsequent years Higginson's road show also touched down at Meadow Brook on Long Island, Shelburne in Vermont, and the Harford Hunt's territory in Maryland.

The Great Foxhound Match, which attracted national attention to foxhunting, came about after Higginson and Harry Worcester Smith, whose Grafton Hounds were also in Massachusetts, had heated exchanges in letters to the editor of *Rider and Driver* as to the relative merits of the English

Mr. Higginson's Hounds in Millbrook's Territory

Collection of Louise W. Mellon,
oil on canvas, 16 by 24 inches, 1922

and American strains of foxhounds. Higginson was a proponent of the former. Through the years he imported some seven hundred hounds from England either for his personal use or for other packs of English foxhounds. Smith, on the other hand, hunted American hounds acquired from hound breeders in Virginia. The match was held in neutral hunting grounds, near Upperville and Middleburg in the Piedmont area of northern Virginia. Judges were appointed, and the two packs alternated in the field for twelve consecutive days. In a split decision, Smith's pack got the nod.

In World War I, Higginson served in the military; he disbanded his pack following the war. In 1931 he moved to England to become the master of the Cattistock Hunt for nine seasons. He also found time to be a prolific author of foxhunting books. He collaborated with his friend Julian Chamberlain in 1928 on the aforementioned *The Hunts of the United States and Canada*, following on his own through the years with *A Tale of Two Foxes*, *The Fox That Walked on Water*, *Peter Beckford, Esq.*, *The Maynell of the West*, *Letters from an Old Sportsman to a Young One*, *As Hounds Ran*, *Try Back*, *Two Centuries of Foxhunting*, and *An Old Sportsman's Memories, 1876–1951*.

Bryce Wing, who made immense contributions to steeplechase racing and foxhunting, and to my life, was a native of New York, where he hunted with the Meadow Brook and Millbrook packs. He moved to Maryland in the early 1930s along with other New Yorkers, including members of the Voss family.

From 1948 to 1964, Bryce served as president of the National Steeplechase & Hunt Association, helping to guide steeplechase racing during challenging times. He also was the chairman of the race committee of the Maryland Hunt Cup, a steward at the racetracks in Maryland, a member of The Jockey Club, and the owner of a small string of steeplechase horses.

In foxhunting, Bryce was the master in the 1930s of the Harford Hunt (now the Elkridge-Harford). His diplomacy, enthusiasm, and experience were of constant value in hunt matters, especially in landowner relations.

Bryce became my stepfather when I was twelve years old. My

S. Bryce Wing

Collection of Margaret K. Mithoefer,
oil on canvas, 28 by 36 inches, 1927

initial days in the hunting field consisted of following Bryce's lead across the lovely Maryland countryside. Likewise, my older brother Garry and I also enjoyed watching Bryce's steeplechase horses train at our farm near Monkton, Maryland, and we cheered for them at the major racetracks and the country race meets up and down the East Coast. A real highlight for Garry and me was, as described in the Seabiscuit section on page 50, attending the War Admiral-Seabiscuit match race at Pimlico in 1938 with Bryce and our mother.

Bryce's love of steeplechasing and foxhunting was ingrained in me in my formative years and has remained throughout my life. He also instilled in me an appreciation of sporting art, especially the work of his close friend and neighbor, Franklin Brooke Voss.

Bryce passed away in 1975 at the age of eighty-five. His granddaughter, Margaret K. Mithoefer, owns the painting of my idol and mentor on his favorite hunter, Whiskey Whiffle.

Tally-Ho

Collection of
Mr. & Mrs. G. Watts Humphrey Jr.,
oil on canvas, 16 by 20 inches, 1939

This is yet another painting of A. Henry Higginson's Middlesex Hounds hunting the Millbrook Hunt territory in New York. Reproduced as *Tally-Ho*, it is one of the four-print series titled "Foxhunting Across America," which Derrydale Press published in 1939. Collectors of sporting art now eagerly seek this series.

S. Bryce Wing, shown in the foreground serving as a whipper-in for Mr. Higginson, described how the painting came about in a 1958 article in *The Chronicle of the Horse*:

Frank was a member of the field that day, but he was about to pull out to catch a train for New York. I persuaded him to wait until we drew the next covert, as it usually held a fox. He did this, and in a short time he heard my halloa from the side of the covert. As he galloped over the hill following hounds, he saw me, cap in hand, viewing the fox. It was a great hunt, lasting an hour and twenty minutes over the best of Millbrook's galloping country. Frank had such a good time that he painted the picture to commemorate the day.

Wing stated that among those who enjoyed the hunt were some of America's most enthusiastic foxhunters. Included were Mr. and Mrs. Edward Carle, Ambrose Clark, Skiddy von Stade, Malcolm Stevenson, O'Malley Knott, Crawford Burton, Dr. and Mrs. Austin Flint, and Oakleigh Thorne, the master of the Millbrook Hunt.

The Millbrook Hunt, one of America's proudest, continues to show excellent sport in Duchess and Columbia counties, some seventy-five miles north of New York City.

This is one of my favorite Voss paintings. It showcases Voss' mastery of animal anatomy, and the picture flows as the viewer's eye follows the hounds from the woods, over the coop, and into the field. It makes you want to be right behind the pack on a good field hunter. Most importantly, the painting is a tribute to huntsman Dallas Leith, who was responsible for creating the Elkridge-Harford's great pack of crossbred foxhounds during Edward S. Voss' years as master.

Leith was born near Middleburg, Virginia, and looked forward to a life of work on his family's farm and to hunting with his father's pack of foxhounds. "I was the sixth generation of my mother's family raised on our farm, which is down the road from Institute Farm [the headquarters of the National Beagle Club]," Leith stated in a 1987 article in *The Chronicle of the Horse*. "From the time I was eight or ten I hunted with my father over parts of the territory of the Middleburg Hunt on days when Middleburg didn't hunt."

Leith's plans changed abruptly, however, in 1930. "One of the whips of the Harford Hunt [now the Elkridge-Harford] was injured in a fall. Their master contacted Daniel C. Sands, the master of the Middleburg Hunt, about a temporary replacement. Mr. Sands asked if I'd be willing to go up to Maryland for a while to help his friend. I thought, 'Oh, for a month or so, I'll do that.'" Dallas Leith stayed put. He was employed by Elkridge-Harford for sixty years and was its huntsman for forty-two years, less three years in the army during World War II.

In 1934 the Harford Hunt merged with the Elkridge Hounds, which had a territory on the outskirts of Baltimore. "There was a vital missing link, though. The hounds weren't all that good at the time," Leith said. "Mr. Howard Bruce, the master of Elkridge, gave me eight hundred dollars to go to Virginia and buy some American dog hounds to breed to our bitches. I purchased hounds from Henry Matthews, who had a farmer pack in the Bull Run

Mountains near Aldie. Matthews always had hounds for sale, and they were the best. My father got hounds from him. So did Mr. Sands and Dr. Randolph [Dr. A.C. Randolph, the master of the Piedmont Fox Hounds]."

Edward S. Voss, who became Elkridge-Harford's master in 1939, was a proponent of English foxhounds; Leith, naturally, of American hounds. They compromised. "Mr. Voss frequently went to England, and he usually brought back a bitch or so, particularly the Duke of Beaufort's stock," Leith said.

In time, Elkridge-Harford's pack of crossbred hounds was acknowledged as one of the best in the United States. Leith retired as Elkridge-Harford's huntsman in 1978 and remained as huntsman emeritus until his death in 1990 at age eighty-two. He has been accorded the highest honor bestowed on American huntsmen — inclusion in the Huntsmen's Room at the Museum of Hounds and Hunting in Leesburg, Virginia.

On a personal note, at age thirteen I hunted behind Dallas Leith in 1939 and on and off for the next thirty-three years. As a kid, I was proud as punch when Dallas, while drawing a covert, occasionally asked me to ride ahead and stand guard at a fox's den. "Don't let him slip in, keep him above ground," Dallas would say. When a little older, I derived great enjoyment from listening with friends to Dallas' little bluegrass band when it played at a local tavern and when Dallas took his guitar to the Bryn Mawr Hound Show to entertain his peers during lunch break.

In addition to being an extraordinary huntsman and hound breeder, Dallas was one of the finest gentlemen I've ever known. Jane Fowler Bassett, a long-time foxhunter with Elkridge-Harford and long-time chairman of the committee responsible for the building and repair of hunt panels throughout the territory, commissioned this painting. Upon her death, it was left to her niece, Mrs. Edward (Binnie) Houghton.

Dallas Leith's Hounds

Collection of Mr. & Mrs. E. Edward Houghton, oil on canvas, 24 by 30 inches, 1944

The Swamp Fox

Collection of Mrs. John D. Schapiro,
oil on canvas, 10 by 14 inches, no date

The Mill Swamp — which is in Elkridge-Harford's hunting territory near the Voss home farm, Atlanta Hall — has held foxes for decades. A fox exiting the swamp was a favorite sight for ardent foxhunter Frank Voss, and I can remember good hunts there as a child, sixty-plus years ago. You can rest assured, too, that Ellie Schapiro, the owner of the painting, has had great fun with swamp foxes in her more than twenty-year tenure as a joint-master of Elkridge-Harford.

In my opinion, *The Swamp Fox* and *Dallas Leith's Hounds* (page 97), in which the hounds are possibly in pursuit of a swamp fox, represent Voss' best work. I get the impression that Voss relished the chance to back off from his usual fare of commissioned portraits of foxhunters and racehorses to do pictures that truly illustrate the joys of his favorite sport.

The Thanksgiving Day meet at St. James Church, in Monkton, Maryland, is an annual highlight for the Elkridge-Harford Hunt. This meet, like many in other parts of the United States, draws a large number of car followers who traditionally enjoy a day in the country prior to their big meal.

Voss' picture has great animation. The artist (center, on foot) is talking with his brother, Edward S. (Ned) Voss, the master of Elkridge-Harford, while his horse (lower left corner) is held by Walter M. Ball, the manager of Ned Voss' hunter stable. Many members of the field are easily identified, notably Jane F. Bassett (foreground, walking to the right). Elsa Voss, wife of the master, is in the left background talking to huntsman Dallas Leith.

Frank Voss was a regular with Elkridge-Harford. As recounted earlier, he died of heart failure at age seventy-three while galloping behind hounds in a hunt several miles from the church. Ned Voss was the master of the hunt for thirty-four years. Ned and Frank are buried at St. James along with other family members and a host of fellow foxhunters.

An Episcopal parish, St. James dates to 1750 and is one of the oldest churches in Maryland. In the summer of 1755, the brick Chapel of Ease (now St. James) was finished at the cost of 790 pounds. The little chapel prospered, and in 1759 an addition was completed at the cost of two hundred pounds.

During the American Revolution, ammunition and weapons were brought to St. James from Baltimore and Annapolis for safe storage. A chapter of the Daughters of the American Revolution donated the plaque that is at the gateway of the churchyard in recognition of the use of the church as an arsenal in 1776.

The church property and most of the land still hunted by Elkridge-Harford are on My Lady's Manor. The book, *St. James of My Lady's Manor, 1750–1950*, colorfully describes the derivation of the name:

Thanksgiving Day Meet in 1943 of the Elkridge-Harford Hunt at St. James Church

Collection of Mrs. William F. Fritz, oil on canvas, 20 by 26 inches, 1944

In the summer of 1667, Charles Calvert, the governor of Maryland, rode on a rare visit to what now are the northern parts of Baltimore County on a mission of peace to the Susquehannock Indians. He saw a sweep of hills, coverts, and rolling meadows whose beauty remained in his memory the rest of his days. Eight years later, Calvert became the third Lord Baltimore. When returning to England, he listed in his name the countryside that so impressed him.

By 1712, Charles had buried three wives and most surely had passed the age of discretion. Apparently, however, he had forgotten its advice, for when he was 75, against all caution, he married for the fourth time. Clinging determinedly to his fast-vanishing dreams and remembrances of youth, he took unto his bride the young and lovely Margaret Charlton of Northumberland, England. In August of 1713, doubtless as a gesture of an old man's effort to tie the frolicsome interests of his girlish wife to him, Lord Baltimore gave to Margaret his 10,000 acres of fair land in his province across the seas to be known as hers forever after as My Lady's Manor.

Louise Lott Bedford, who died in 1978 at age seventy-six, moved to Maryland from New York with her husband, Dean, in the 1920s. The lovely, rolling countryside north of Baltimore near the Pennsylvania line, ideal for foxhunting, attracted the Bedfords and a number of other New Yorkers to an area that is still hunted by the Elkridge-Harford Hunt, which celebrated its 125th anniversary in 2003.

Mr. and Mrs. Bedford both were masters at one time or another of the Elkridge-Harford, and they also enjoyed foot hunting with their private pack, the Pemberton Beagles. Mrs. Bedford was a marvelous equestrian who shared her knowledge and enthusiasm with youngsters. In 1954 she was the founder with Alexander Mackay-Smith and Colonel Howard Fair of the U.S. Pony Clubs Inc., which now has more than 14,000 members.

An article by Mackay-Smith in *The Chronicle of the Horse* in 1952 explained Mrs. Bedford's contributions to youth:

Mrs. Bedford has for years been developing young foxhunters … As a result, those who go hunting with Elkridge are apt to find a whole covey of young fry scampering along on ponies after hounds and well up in the first flight, taking fences as they come … Her work with the children of Maryland has become a byword for which all of us who are looking to the future of American riding can be grateful.

I was raised on a farm that adjoined the Bedfords' Fox Hill Farm.

Louise Lott Bedford

Collection of Cricket Bedford Whitner,
oil on canvas, 18 by 24 inches, 1952

My childhood predated the founding of the Pony Club, but I was fortunate to be a member of Mrs. Bedford's "covey of young fry," as were my closest friends, Paddy and Mikey Smithwick. The Smithwicks became legends in steeplechasing: Paddy as a champion jockey, Mikey as a leading trainer. Both brothers are members of the Racing Hall of Fame in Saratoga Springs, New York. For my part, I am indebted to Louise Bedford and to my stepfather, Bryce Wing, for igniting in me as a child an interest in foxhunting that exists to this day, some sixty-five years later.

After moving from Maryland to Virginia in 1972, I frequently hunted with the Piedmont Fox Hounds, for which Mrs. Bedford's son, Erskine, was a longtime master. He was as enthusiastic a foxhunter as I've ever known and the best field master I've ever hunted behind. He made hunting fun for everyone and, like his mother, enjoyed accompanying children in the field. Unfortunately, he was killed by a fall in the hunting field at age sixty-five.

Voss' portrait catches Mrs. Bedford exactly as I remember her. Her facial expression and seat are perfect, and I enjoy her being turned out in leggings and a derby hat, which are foreign to today's horsewomen. I like, too, the fact that the horse isn't picture perfect, that one ear is cocked back. Thanks, Frank Voss, for the memories; thanks, Louise Bedford, for what you have meant to me.

The Elkridge-Harford Hunt Crossing Atlanta Hall Meadow

Collection of Thomas H. Voss,
oil on canvas, 28 by 38 inches, 1942

Elkridge-Harford, Elkridge-Harford, Elkridge-Harford. You must be getting tired of the name, but bear with me; this is the final reproduction dealing with Frank Voss' favorite hunt in this book of paintings. I promise.

The painting is of (left to right) huntsman Dallas Leith; Edward S. (Ned) Voss, master of foxhounds; and whipper-in Jake Robinson with Elkridge-Harford's pack of crossbred hounds in the incredibly beautiful meadow on Edward Voss' Atlanta Hall Farm in Monkton, Maryland. The Sporting Gallery and Bookshop of New York marketed an edition of 250 signed prints of the painting in 1943. I'm the proud owner of print number twenty-eight.

Here I go getting personal again, but I can't refrain because the scene means so much to me. It isn't just that I've ridden and hunted countless times over this meadow. You see, a few years ago Tom Voss — the grandson of Edward Voss and great-nephew of Frank Voss — and my brother Garry, who was Tom's godfather, jointly owned the very successful steeplechase horse Cookie. As a pensioner, Cookie was pastured in the meadow at Atlanta Hall when he was killed by lightning. He's buried under the tree where this happened. Garry died in 2000; his ashes were spread at Cookie's grave.

Voss' incredibly detailed painting shows the Meadow Brook Hunt's Thanksgiving Day meet in 1923 at Woodside Acres, the estate of Mr. and Mrs. James A. Burden, built in 1917 at Syosset, Long Island. Designed by prominent architect William A. Delano, the mansion won architectural awards and was featured in *Architectural Record* in 1923. That summer the house was loaned to the Prince of Wales as his base during a visit to the United States. The estate is now the site of the Woodcrest Country Club.

Peter Villa, a well-established dealer in sporting art in New York City, identified a number of the foxhunters in the painting. Mrs. Burden is in the left foreground, riding sidesaddle. Huntsman Thomas Allison is on the dark bay with hounds, and Harry I. Nicholas, the joint master of Meadow Brook, is on Allison's left, riding the chestnut. Katharine Redmond is on the gray horse in the left background, while the tiny figures on foot in front of the mansion are Mr. Burden

Thanksgiving Day Meet in 1923 of the Meadow Brook Hunt

Private collection, oil on canvas, 32 by 42 inches, 1923

and daughter Adele. Edward S. Voss, the artist's brother, is doffing his hat to Mrs. W. Goadby Loew. The lady riding astride in the right foreground is the Burdens' daughter, Sheila, twenty at the time. To her right is Harry T. Peters, who is chatting with Mrs. Nicholas. The group to their right includes the artist. Among the other members of the field are William Langley, Devereux Milburn, Malcolm Stevenson, Frank Appleton, Egerton Winthrop, Betty Babcock, and Harvey Ladew, a veritable Who's Who of socially prominent sportsmen in the golden age of sport on Long Island.

In 1926, when Voss was in England to hunt with his friend the Duke of Beaufort, a photograph of the Burdens' painting was shown, prompting the Duke to commission Voss to paint hounds passing in front of his Badminton House. England's famous three-day event is held at Badminton. Prints of the painting became available in England, which paved the way for a number of commissions for Voss.

Katharine Redmond, who was one of America's most enthusiastic and skilled horsewomen in the decades before and after World War II, lived on Long Island, which was then one of the most important centers of horse sports in the United States. The Piping Rock Club held important horse shows, the Meadow Brook Club hosted international polo in addition to quality foxhunting and timber racing, and nearby Belmont Park was the site of championship flat racing and steeplechasing. This was indeed the heyday of sport on Long Island, where Redmond's family joined the Hitchcocks, Belmonts, Clarks, von Stades, Morgans, Bostwicks, and other families in enjoying the sporting life to the fullest.

Mrs. Redmond, whose maiden name was Register, married Norman Toerge after the death of her first husband, Geraldyn Livingston Redmond. For the purpose of this piece, I will refer to her as Mrs. Redmond.

In addition to Gray Horse Farm on Long Island (named for her love of gray horses), Katharine Redmond had a winter residence in Aiken, South Carolina, and a farm, Little Cotland, in The Plains, Virginia. An ardent foxhunter, she was in the first flight with hunts throughout America, particularly Meadow Brook, Aiken, and Virginia's Orange County. She is shown here on one of her hunters, Calatrava, over a fence with Meadow Brook in 1928.

In the early 1930s Mrs. Redmond won the first horse race in America restricted to lady riders, the Diana Stakes in Aiken. This seemed to fire the emotions of Harry Worcester Smith, an ardent

Katharine Redmond

Collection of Nancy Redmond Manierre,
oil on canvas, 26 by 44 inches, 1928

foxhunter and leader in steeplechasing as an owner and rider. Smith also was the author of *Life and Sport in Aiken* and other prestigious books. Then in his sixties, Smith enclosed a lengthy letter with his 1932 Christmas card to the attractive young race rider. In part it read:

Dear Mrs. Redmond: Here's my Christmas card and among Will Ogilive's poems I found one the other day especially applicable to you titled 'Fair Girls and Gray Horses.'

The poem includes the following stanza:

A toast for you, who never went wide of a fence or a kiss.

While horses are horses and eyes are blue, there's never a toast in the world like this.

Smith, obviously quite a ladies' man in addition to being a skilled horseman and journalist, concluded his letter with the following paragraph:

When the season is in full swing, I hope the Thursday drags [at Aiken] *will be as fast as days of old, when one of my happiest thoughts was to always find your blue eyes and curly hair bang up at the finish.*

Dashing expressions, I must say, and Voss' painting, equally emotive, is one of his few paintings in which the subject is jumping a fence. The painting's owner, Nancy Redmond Manierre, proudly points out that besides her mother; her late husband, Cyrus; and herself, two other generations of her family currently enjoy sport with the Orange County Hunt: her daughter-in-law Betsy Manierre, a three-day-a-week foxhunter, and her grandson, Redmond Livingston (Stony) Manierre Jr.

Voss' painting of the master and staff of the Meadow Brook Hunt was commissioned by the hunt's master, Harry T. Peters, in 1930, when the Long Island hunt enjoyed an era known for good sport and extravagant living. The Great Depression slowed this era, and it ended with the urbanization of Meadow Brook's hunting country following World War II. The figures in the painting include Peters (second from left) and Thomas Allison (third from left), who was Meadow Brook's huntsman from 1911 through 1951. The whipper-in at the far right is Charlie Plumb, who rode Alligator to win important timber races. The Burden estate at Syosset was the site of the painting.

Meadow Brook's proud heritage dates to the early 1880s, when foxhunters in and around New York City had several options for enjoying their sport. They could take a ferry to Staten Island to join the Richmond County Hounds. On the north shore of Long Island, the Queens County Hounds was the popular hunt, and the same pertained to the Rockaway Hunt on the south shore. Yet another choice was to hunt with the Essex County Hunt in northern New Jersey.

Some of Queens County's members broke away in 1881 to found Meadow Brook, which in short order became one of the most prestigious hunts in the United States. Early on, members like Edwin Morgan and Thomas Hitchcock Sr., who was the master from 1889 to 1892, purchased farmland at bargain prices around Westbury. They retained some properties and sold others to New Yorkers for weekend retreats.

The New York newspapers soon began to carry accounts of Meadow Brook's sport, and the Long Island Railroad adjusted its schedule to accommodate the foxhunters. As reported in *The History of American Foxhunters, Volume II*, August Belmont Jr., the master in 1884, sent the following notice to club members:

The Long Island Rail Road has extended the 1:05 p.m. train from Long Island City, which runs now only as far as Jamaica, on to Hempstead, reaching the latter place at 1:50 p.m. on all days when the Meadow Brook Hounds meet. This regulation thus renders all the meets conveniently accessible.

Theodore Roosevelt, then in his twenties, described in *Century Magazine* a drag hunt with Meadow Brook in 1886 from the Roosevelt estate, Sagamore Hill, in Oyster Bay:

We ran for almost ten miles at a rattling pace with only two checks, crossing somewhat more than sixty fences, stiff as steel … A good many falls took place, resulting in an unusual percentage of accidents. The Master dislocated one knee, another broke two ribs and another — the present writer — broke his arm.

Roosevelt stated that the broken arm didn't hurt at all, that he continued and was present at the end. Good preparation, I'd say, for Roosevelt's big game hunting, the charge up San Juan Hill, and the "Big Stick" policy during his presidency.

Allison and Peters, who embarked upon a long tenure as master in 1925, greatly enhanced the quality of Meadow Brook's sport. Allison brought hounds from his native Virginia and proved that live hunting could be enjoyed despite the challenge of poor scenting on Long Island's sandy soil. Peters was a perfectionist and knowledgeable of every facet of foxhunting. He expressed his thoughts in his book, *Just Hunting*, published in 1935. He was also America's foremost collector and expert on prints by Currier & Ives, and he wrote a book on this passion.

The Meadow Brook Grays

Collection of Katrina H. Becker,
oil on canvas, 24 by 36 inches, 1930

Dr. A.C. (Archie) Randolph, a medical doctor who devoted a large part of his life to foxhunting and being the master of the Piedmont Fox Hounds in Upperville, Virginia, once told a friend: "Birthing [babies] and foxhunting each takes pretty much a full day. I'd rather go foxhunting." And the latter is precisely what Dr. Randolph did for a total of twenty-six years as Piedmont's leader, until Parkinson's disease forced him to step down in 1954.

Alexander Mackay-Smith, an avid foxhunter who was editor of *The Chronicle of the Horse* magazine from 1949 to 1974, wrote about Voss' painting of Dr. Randolph when it appeared on the cover of the *Chronicle* in 1950:

Frank Voss has done one of his finest works in his painting of Dr. Randolph. Those of us who have hunted with the Piedmont Fox Hounds will instantly recognize the familiar figure of its master and his grand old hunter Ranter. From the splendid facial likeness to every

Dr. Archibald Cary Randolph

Collection of Shelby W. Bonnie, oil on canvas, 28 by 36 inches, 1947

detail of the manner in which he sits on a horse, and to Ranter himself, the artist from Maryland has made a superb painting ... He has painted Dr. Randolph and Ranter with an impressive background of some of Piedmont's best country. It is a sweep well known to Piedmont followers, for hounds have found and pursued many a fox through the midst of it. Here, there is a variety of fences: stone walls predominate in the northern section while the southern part has many flights of timber rails, particularly over Paul Mellon's Rokeby Farm ... Ranter was regularly hunted by Dr. Randolph for fourteen years. He is a great field hunter that fits well the tradition behind the hunting country and its sporting master.

I am glad to say that the tradition carries on at Piedmont, where topnotch sport continues to be shown. As the successor to Mackay-Smith as editor of the *Chronicle*, I have had the opportunity to hunt occasionally with Piedmont and report on the fun in the *Chronicle*.

Theodora Ayer Randolph was a leader in horse showing, horse breeding, and steeplechase racing. She is best remembered in foxhunting circles as the master of the Piedmont Fox Hounds for forty-two years, commencing in 1954 upon the retirement of her husband, Dr. A.C. Randolph. During her tenure Piedmont became one of the finest hunts in America. Such was her fervor for the sport that she once went foxhunting with either her own or neighboring packs on thirty consecutive days. "My streak would have gone on, but I had to go Christmas shopping," she told a friend.

Many of Mrs. Randolph's horses were champions either in the show ring or on the racecourse. Her Bon Nouvel was the U.S. champion steeplechaser in 1964, 1965, and 1968. His most awesome race was in the Temple Gwathmey Handicap at Aqueduct in 1965, when he carried 170 pounds to win by thirty lengths. He is a member of the Racing Hall of Fame.

Mrs. Randolph was an excellent judge of a young person's potential. She often took aspiring young horsemen under her wing and backed them through good times and bad. In horse showing she supported show jumping riders Rodney Jenkins, now a prominent trainer of flat horses, and Kathy Kusner, who rode in the Olympics. In racing, some of her favorites were Paddy and Mikey Smithwick, who are members of the Racing Hall of Fame for their accomplishments in steeplechasing; Tommy Smith, the winner of the English Grand National on Jay Trump; and Billy Turner, the trainer of Seattle Slew.

Mrs. Randolph enjoyed the nickname "The Kingfish," bestowed on her many years ago by steeplechase jockey George Bland. The story goes that Mrs. Randolph was dressed to the nines when she stopped by the stables before the races one day at Saratoga. "You're struttin' like a kingfish," said Bland. The name stuck.

Mrs. Randolph was highly opinionated and outspoken; you knew exactly where she stood on any question. The illegal use of performance-enhancing drugs in horse showing and racing was an issue about which she was particularly adamant. Her opposition to such use was one of many reasons that the American Horse Shows Association selected her for a lifetime achievement award in 1996, several months before she passed away at the age of ninety.

"The Kingfish" was quite a lady. Her painting hangs at Oakley, Mrs. Randolph's former home near Upperville. Her grandson Shelby Bonnie, who is one of the masters of the Piedmont Fox Hounds, now owns Oakley.

Theodora Ayer Randolph

Collection of Shelby W. Bonnie,
oil on canvas, 24 by 30 inches, 1947

As a youth in his native Maryland, W. Plunket Stewart hunted a pack of foxhounds with his elder brother Redmond. In 1892 Redmond Stewart founded the Green Spring Valley Hounds, hunting the hounds himself with Plunket as his whipper-in. The Stewart brothers also enjoyed riding in steeplechase races. In 1898 Plunket won the Maryland Hunt Cup, while Redmond rode the second horse to finish. In 1904 Redmond was the winner with Plunket just behind him.

With Redmond Stewart hunting the Green Spring country and his brother-in-law, Frank A. Bonsal Sr., hunting the neighboring country to the north, the choice hunting territories in Maryland were spoken for. Consequently, Plunket Stewart, whose ambition since childhood was to have his own pack of hounds and a territory in which to hunt them, cast his eyes to the north, focusing on an expanse of lovely rolling countryside near Unionville, just across the Mason-Dixon Line in southeastern Pennsylvania, twenty miles northwest of Wilmington, Delaware. Stewart described his search in A. Henry Higginson and Julian Ingersoll's book *Hunting in the United States and Canada*, published in 1928:

In 1911 and 1912, I found myself scouring Chester and Delaware counties by motor looking for such a country, which would be available and not be an interference to an existing recognized hunt … One day I happened to be bumping along the road that runs from Unionville to Doe Run. The beauty of the country and the splendid footing afforded by the fine old sod fields made me suddenly realize that here was the country that I would like to have … I obtained the consent of Mr. Charles E. Mather, who controlled the Brandywine country immediately to the east, and in 1912 I bought my first property of 211 acres known as Chesterland.

W. Plunket Stewart

Collection of Mrs. John B. Hannum,
oil on canvas, 32 by 38 inches, 1935

Stewart named his hunt Mr. Stewart's Cheshire Foxhounds. The Higginson/Ingersoll book explained the choice of Cheshire in the title: *It [Cheshire] was old English for Chester as in Chester County. Mr. Stewart prefixed his own name to differentiate his hunt from England's Cheshire Hunt.*

Higginson and Ingersoll were lavish in their praise of Stewart's hunting country:

There are many small coverts, and foxes, once started, are apt to make long points. Moreover, Pennsylvania is a foxhunting state, and the farmers know and love the sport, which is with them as much a tradition as it is in England.

Nancy Mohr stated in her book, *The Lady Blows the Horn* (a biography of Stewart's stepdaughter, America's premier female huntsman Nancy Hannum), that Plunket Stewart offered farmers fair prices for their land along with lifetime tenancy and put cash on the kitchen table to seal deals. He would then either add the land to his holdings or sell it to a person who liked foxhunting and open spaces. In short order, Stewart developed a pack of English foxhounds that gave excellent sport, as good as any pack in the United States. Stewart also became a national leader in foxhunting as the president of the Masters of Foxhounds Association from 1938 until his death in 1948.

The Chronicle of the Horse editor Stacy Lloyd wrote in Stewart's obituary:

This was no ordinary man. He was one of the greatest sportsmen of his era, one who made the Cheshire Hounds a household name among those who hold a foxhound dear, and one who had strict adherence to a code of sportsmanship too little practiced nowadays. He kept a standard flying high, a standard seldom seen elsewhere.

The painting *Mr. Stewart's Cheshire Foxhounds*, commissioned in 1947, honored W. Plunket Stewart for his thirty-four years as Cheshire's master. Huntsman Charlie Smith is at the left with Cheshire's pack of English foxhounds, while whipper-in Oscar Crossan is in the background. Stewart is in the foreground, followed by his wife, Carol, and Stewart's stepdaughters, Nancy Hannum and Avie Walker.

Nancy Penn Smith Hannum became the master of Cheshire upon the death of the hunt's founder in 1948. This piece on Cheshire's history focuses on Hannum, who brought to Cheshire a rich heritage in foxhunting. Her father, Richard (Buzzy) Penn Smith, like Stewart a lifelong foxhunter, was the master of the now defunct Chester Valley Hunt in Pennsylvania and a joint-master of the Orange County Hunt in Virginia for several years prior to his death from pneumonia in 1929 at age thirty-six. Hannum's mother, Carol Penn Smith — a sister of W. Averell Harriman, governor of New York and ambassador to Russia — also served for two seasons as Orange County's joint-master. After Penn Smith's death, she married Plunket Stewart.

Hounds and hunting have always been a part of Nancy Hannum's life. As a child she hunted with Orange County, and she was the huntsman of a pack of beagles while a student at Foxcroft School, and, of course, a regular in her stepfather's tenure at Cheshire. She commenced hunting the hounds herself shortly after taking over the Cheshire mastership, becoming a huntsman of limitless skill and dedication, enabling the quality of the sport to rise to new heights. In 1978 members of the hunt honored Hannum on her thirtieth year as master. Words by long-time foxhunter Edgar Scott Jr. marked the occasion: "I think it's generally agreed that whatever Mrs. Hannum does, she does with strength and vigor."

In addition to being America's foremost female huntsman, Hannum brought strength and vigor to other aspects of her life, whether in land conservation or training horses for steeplechase racing. Involvement in preserving the countryside earned Hannum and her hunt the Hunting Habitat Conservation Award from the Masters of Foxhounds Association in 1997. *The Chronicle of the Horse* editor John Strassburger, in covering the award ceremony for the magazine, wrote:

Mrs. Hannum has taken a highly personal, labor-intensive approach to maintaining Cheshire's hunt country as one of the world's finest. She has never shied away from cajoling, pleading with or chiding landowners to leave as much of the thick hardwood forests, open grasslands covering rolling hills, and sprawling cornfields as natural as possible.

Hannum's goal in training steeplechase horses was success in the Maryland Hunt Cup with horses that were hunted with Cheshire. Her husband, John B. Hannum, formerly a federal judge, rode in four Hunt Cups, with two seconds and a third; her son, Richard Penn Smith (Buzzy) Hannum, won the Hunt Cup in 1970 and 1973 on the homebred Morning Mac; another son, John B. (Jock) Hannum Jr., won many point-to-points and was a close second in the 1987 Hunt Cup. Her daughter Carol Davidson was an accomplished rider in timber races for lady riders and in combined training events.

Although Hannum stepped down as Cheshire's huntsman in 1982 due to a number of injuries from falls in the hunting field, she continued as master through the 2003 season. This made for an incredible ninety-year tenure of mastership for Plunket Stewart and his stepdaughter, a record in American foxhunting. Nancy Hannum is surely the first lady of American foxhunting, a legend in her lifetime.

Mr. Stewart's Cheshire Foxhounds

Collection of Mrs. John B. Hannum,
oil on canvas, 32 by 40 inches, 1947

Ann Van Nest Gambrill of Peapack, New Jersey, was a regular with the Essex Fox Hounds before and after World War II, riding her lovely Thoroughbred hunter, Silver Fox. They also enjoyed sport in the winter months with the Aiken Hounds in South Carolina.

It is appropriate that a lady should go well with Essex. The roots of this fine hunt date to 1876 with the founding of the Montclair Equestrian Club, about thirty miles north of the hunt's present site in Peapack. According to a description in *The History of American Foxhunting, Volume II*, the club's founder was "an enthusiastic lady equestrian, the daughter of an English family living in Montclair." The club's membership consisted of "young ladies fond of exercise in the saddle."

Successively, the Equestrian Club became the Montclair Hunt (1878), the Essex County Hunt (1890, the private hunt of Charles Pfizer) and, finally, the Essex Fox Hounds in 1912.

In the late 1890s, the youngster Gordon Grand, who became America's foremost author of foxhunting fiction with books such as

Ann Van Nest Gambrill

Collection of Anne Casey van den Bergh, oil on canvas, 14 by 18 inches, 1942

The Silver Horn and *Old Man*, commenced hunting with Essex. In the preface to his book, *A Horse for Christmas Morning and Other Stories*, Grand reminisced:

Harking back in my memory, I am impressed with how hard some of us labored in those days to get a bit of hunting. Being unable because of school to get out with hounds other than on Saturdays, my procedure was as follows: Upon getting excused from school early on Thursdays, I would hack Ranger, my one and only horse, the thirty-two miles from my home in the Oranges to the kennels at Gladstone, taking a somewhat circuitous route in quest of soft roads. I then got myself back to the Oranges as best I could. Ranger rested on Fridays, and on the following Saturday I would travel to Newark and connect with a train to Gladstone. After hunting on Saturdays, I would spend the night in the country, get up at the crack of dawn and ride that gay, courageous little horse the thirty-two miles back to the Oranges.

Today's foxhunters at Essex have seemingly inherited Grand's zest and determination, having kept the sport alive and well in a hunting territory that is only fifty miles from New York City.

Chapter Six

Miscellaneous Subjects

A Girl and Her Pony

Collection of Mrs. John D. Schapiro,
oil on canvas, 14 by 20 inches, 1926

This delightful portrait of a young equestrian reflects the artist's mastery of equine anatomy and his uncanny ability to paint landscapes. Sadly, however, identification of the subject has not been made. I'm certain that, upon this book's publication, yours truly will receive a call from a miffed descendant of the subject. Mrs. Schapiro's late husband John, the former president of Laurel Park and creator of the Washington, D.C., International, bought the painting at a Sotheby's auction some years ago.

F. Ambrose Clark, who died in 1964 at age eighty-three, was an equestrian Renaissance man. In addition to being a crack four-in-hand whip, he was a foxhunter, steeplechase jockey and owner, race meeting director, and collector of sporting art and books. His interests were typically English; he even resembled an eighteenth-century English country squire.

Clark's grandfather, New York City attorney Edward Clark, created the fortune that made this lifestyle possible by forming a partnership in the 1800s with Isaac Merritt Singer, who had obtained a patent for the first sewing machine. Singer lacked business acumen; Clark's financial and promotional skills made the Singer Sewing Machine Co. one of the largest companies in the world at the time.

However, Ambrose paid no attention to money management. A lifelong friend, S. Bryce Wing, quoted Clark in Clark's obituary in *The Chronicle of the Horse*: "I'm not a money maker. All I know is horses. Why should I go puttering down to an office to meddle in something another man can do a hundred times better?"

Clark had estates on Long Island at Westbury, at Cooperstown in upstate New York, and in Aiken, South Carolina. He also had a townhouse in New York and a mansion in Melton Mowbray, his foxhunting headquarters in England.

Broad Hollow, the estate on Long Island, housed Clark's extensive art collection, which art critic E.J. Rousack described in an introduction in *The F. Ambrose Clark Collection of Sporting Paintings*:

The collection is dispersed through the handsome country home,

which looks out on green paddocks where horses pasture, and on a splendid stable and carriage house. There is no discontinuity between outdoors and in. Many of the pictures painted by the great sporting masters hanging on the walls can be glimpsed out of the windows. The master of the collection might be one of the squires and country gentlemen painted with their hounds and horses two hundred years ago.

Clark's collection included paintings by such English masters as Alken, Ferneley, Herring, Marshall, Munnings, and Stubbs. Also, Clark had three pictures by his good friend Frank Voss.

The Meadow Brook Cup, a race over timber fences first run in 1883, was held at Broad Hollow from 1926 through 1941. George F.T. Ryall wrote in *Country Life* magazine in 1935:

Ambrose Clark likes to give picnics. The Meadow Brook race meeting, of which he is president, is his favorite picnic. Weeks before the races, he tinkers over the fences, although they always are in perfect condition, and on race day he is everywhere, leading the parade to the post on his pony, patrolling the course and presenting the trophies.

Upon Clark's death, his widow, Florence, gave Bryce Wing the choice of any piece in the art collection in memory of his great friend. Wing chose Voss' four-in-hand painting. "It has great meaning to me, brings back memories," Wing said. " 'Brose is the whip, and I'm seated just behind, in the gray hat."

Upon his death in 1975, Bryce Wing left the painting to me, his stepson.

F. Ambrose Clark Driving to the Meadow Brook Club for Polo

Collection of Peter Winants, oil on canvas, 12 by 16 inches, 1927

So much has been written of J. Watson Webb's contributions to foxhunting that it's easy to overlook his participation in high-goal polo. Webb embarked on the sport at an early age by stick and balling at his family's Shelburne Farms in Vermont, on homebred horses that were too small for foxhunting. The Hackney Barn at Shelburne had tanbark footing and was large enough for indoor polo. Webb pursued his interest at Yale, where he was on the polo team in 1906 and 1907.

Between 1914 and 1925, Webb was a member of the winning team in the U.S. Polo Championships five times, and he played on the American team that defeated England in international matches in 1921, 1924, and 1927. In the 1921 match he teamed with Louis Stoddard Sr., Thomas Hitchcock Jr., and Devereux Milburn. The 1924 and 1927 teams consisted of Hitchcock, Milburn, Webb, and Malcolm Stevenson. In the book *American Polo*, author Newell Bent described the 1927 team as "one of the greatest — perhaps the very greatest ever — polo team this world has ever seen."

The records are sketchy, but Webb was surely one of the very

Polo at Meadow Brook

Collection of Shelburne Museum, watercolor, 11½ by 11½ inches, 1927

few left-handed polo players to attain a ten-goal rating, the highest USPA handicap. Playing left-handed is no longer allowed. In 1974 the USPA mandated, for safety concerns, that the sport be restricted to right-handed players. The rationale for the change is evident in Voss' painting, where both players have their mallets on the right side of their horses and away from each other. Depending on the players' position on the field, the mallets of a right- and a left-handed player could be in between the horses, creating possible injury.

A letter from Webb's son, Samuel, to Webb's granddaughter, Kitty Webb Harris, is attached to the reverse of Voss' painting:

Dear Kitty:

The watercolor of your grandfather [left] *and Devereux Milburn was done at the Open Championship Tournament at Meadow Brook, Long Island, in 1927 … I think Frank Voss, who knew all of us well, had a lapse of memory, because I would say he has* [your] *grandpa holding the mallet in his right hand!*

Much love, Uncle Sam

Whatever the case, this watercolor is noteworthy in that Voss rarely did action pictures, and he seldom worked in this medium.

A Hunter with His Groom

Collection of Edmund T. Mudge IV,
oil on canvas, 16 by 20 inches, 1930

Although the subject is not identified, this painting is simply too good to leave out. The expression of the groom reflects pride in his horse, and his attire reflects pride in his profession. Also, the composition is superb — the oak trees frame the subject and the stone wall further creates depth, leading us to the woods in the background.

If you've read the essay on Louise Bedford in the foxhunting chapter, I'm certain you've gotten the idea that Dean and Louise Bedford were involved in a wide assortment of activities associated with country living. Together, they did it all; you'd see one, you'd see the other, whether it was Pony Club, riding for the handicapped, foxhunting, horse showing, raising Norwich terriers, you name it. There was an exception, though — the Pemberton Beagles. Beagling was Dean Bedford's thing. It was his pack. He was the creator, the caretaker, and the huntsman. Mrs. Bedford was only marginally involved, as a whipper-in on hunting days.

Dean Bedford's father, A.C. Bedford, the chairman of the Standard Oil Company of New Jersey, owned the estate, Pemberton, near Westbury, Long Island. When the couple first married in the early 1920s, Dean and Louise lived on a part of the estate. Upon moving to Maryland later that decade, they turned their plan to develop a pack of foot hounds named for their former home into a reality. The Pemberton Beagles hunted portions of Elkridge-Harford Hunt's territory. To enhance the sport, Bedford imported a number of jackrabbits from Kansas. The jacks

The Pemberton Beagles

Collection of Dean Bedford Jr.,
oil on canvas, 28 by 36 inches, 1930

were far larger and faster than the cottontails that are native to the area. The jackrabbits often ran flat-out across the countryside, rather than in circles like the smaller bunnies, giving great sport. However, they didn't flourish in their new environment and became increasingly scarce. The pack again had to settle for cottontails.

Dean Bedford firmly believed that the best way to learn about hunting was on foot, in intimate contact with hounds. I remember as a child that the Bedfords encouraged participation by youngsters in the community. However, most of us dug our feet in, far preferring to gallop madly on our ponies across the countryside behind foxhounds, not having a clue about hound work. On foot with beagles? No way, except on occasional Sundays when hunt teas followed hunting.

On a very personal — and trivial — note, I can blame one of the teas for a lifelong aversion to fruitcake. I stuffed myself, with dire results. Today, though, there's no aversion with regard to beagling. I occasionally enjoy sport in Virginia with the Wolver Beagles, and I now concur with Dean Bedford: there's no better way to learn about hunting.

That Liz Whitney Tippett marched to her own band is reflected in her portrait, painted at her Llangollen Farm near Upperville, Virginia, in 1931. At the time she was twenty-five and the recent bride of international sportsman John Hay (Jock) Whitney. While most of the paintings in this book show subjects attired in their "Sunday best," Liz chose informality to the extent that she's riding bareback, and a halter and lead shank replaced a bridle on champion show hunter Grey Knight.

Voss' painting captures an incredibly lovely lady in equally beautiful surroundings. The painting has great depth, with a stately oak on the left framing the subject, and in the middle distance, a pasture, fence line, and trees lead the viewer to the Blue Ridge Mountains in the background.

When Liz died in 1989 at age eighty-two, her obituary in *The Blood-Horse* captured the "own band" theme:

Liz Whitney Tippett left her many friends and acquaintances with a variety of memories. They remembered that she landed in the infield of Hollywood Park in a purple helicopter [her racing colors], had arrived one morning [at the stables] at Saratoga dressed in a fur coat and evening gown, had auditioned for the role of Scarlett O'Hara in 'Gone With the Wind,' had hosted parties attended by movie stars and heads of state, and had treated her dogs and horses like children. As the striking debutante, the lucky bride and the talked-about divorcee, Mrs. Tippett made good stories for newspapers and created memories for the people who knew her.

Ten thousand onlookers attended Liz's wedding in 1930 to Whitney, whose ushers included Fred Astaire, polo great Tommy Hitchcock Jr., and the bridegroom's cousin, C.V. Whitney. Liz's bridesmaids included the groom's sister, Joan Whitney Payson, and Astaire's sister, Adele. For a wedding present, Jock gave Liz the two-thousand-acre Llangollen Farm ("land's end" in Welsh) and

one million dollars. At Llangollen the Whitneys built a steeple-chase course that resembled in difficulty the English Grand National. Twenty thousand spectators attended the first meet in 1931.

The Whitneys divorced in 1940. Liz maintained friendships with Hollywood idols such as Robert Mitchum, Jane Russell, Zsa Zsa Gabor, John Wayne, and Ingrid Bergman, while Elizabeth Taylor was particularly close. Through the years, Liz named racehorses for some of her Hollywood friends. Liz Taylor was a stakes winner.

In 1948 Liz married Dr. E. Cooper Person, who died in 1952. Two years later she married Richard Dwight Lunn, whom she divorced after five years. She enjoyed an excellent marriage, however, with Colonel Cloyce Tippett. Married in 1960, the Tippetts shared interests in country living, carriage driving, and world travel for twenty-eight years, until Liz's death.

The biggest coup in Liz's sixty years in Thoroughbred racing was importing Argentinean champion Endeavor II in 1947. Endeavor II became an excellent stakes winner in this country. At stud, he sired Porterhouse, the first stakes winner saddled by Charlie Whittingham, who became a Hall of Fame trainer. Porterhouse, a champion at two, won stakes races until age six for Llangollen. In 1960 Liz opened a Florida division of Llangollen, where Pretense, a son of Endeavor II, was foaled. Pretense won six stakes races in 1963, including the Gulfstream Park and Santa Anita handicaps.

Colonel Tippett passed away in 1994. Roy L. Ash now owns Llangollen, which has been restored to its former grandeur. The Piedmont Fox Hounds sometimes have meets there, and the stables are leased to a trainer of steeplechase horses. Liz Whitney Tippett would approve, and she would also approve that Mrs. Paul Mellon, one of her closest friends, now owns the painting.

Liz Whitney Tippett

Collection of Mrs. Paul Mellon,
oil on canvas, 28 by 36 inches, 1931

R ichard Van Nest Gambrill, who died in 1954 at age sixty-four, was one of America's most committed sportsmen in the golden age of sport. He was a leader in coaching, beagling, foxhunting, steeplechasing, golf, and yachting.

Frank Voss' painting depicts Gambrill on the box of his coach and four-in-hand in the yard at Vernon Manor Stables, Peapack, New Jersey, about fifty miles west of New York City. Gambrill procured the team, known as the Vanderbilt Grays, from close friend William Vanderbilt, an international figure in driving and, like Gambrill, a member of the Coaching Club of America.

Gambrill and his wife Ann were regulars with the nearby Essex Fox Hounds. At right in the background of the painting is Mrs. Gambrill's field hunter, John O'Gaunt. The kennel for the Vernon Somerset Beagles, of which Gambrill was the founder and huntsman, is not seen in the painting.

Vernon Manor Stables is detailed in the book *Sporting Stables and Kennels*, co-authored by Gambrill and James C. Mackenzie, the architect who designed Vernon Manor and other stables in an era known for grand stables. Derrydale Press published the book in 1935. The stable complex had fifteen box stalls, a carriage house, tack and harness rooms, a trophy room, a farrier shop, washrooms, and the stud groom's cottage. Grooms quarters were on the second floor of the exquisite brick structure, along with storage for hay and straw.

Twenty-five years ago Gambrill's descendants sold the family mansion, stables, and forty acres. "There are no horses there now," said Gambrill's granddaughter, Anne van den Bergh. "However, we're pleased that great care has been given to the stables. One could move in with a string of horses and be right at home, just as in my grandfather's time."

Van den Bergh was five when her grandfather passed away, but the stable, run by headman Murray McIver, was maintained for ten or so years. She recalled times spent there as a young girl:

I can remember Vernon Manor in its heyday. I knew every nook and corner, and was particularly impressed with the tack and harness rooms, with leather shining like pennies, framed by hunting prints, photos, and ribbons. I also fondly remember Murray, a Scotsman who was a marvelous horseman and had a great sense of humor. In all, there were nine of us grandchildren, all living in the vicinity. Murray taught this gang to ride, first at the walk and trot in the yard, then out into the woods to pop over little logs. It was an adventure; invariably, several of the clan would be on ponies with mouths of iron, taking off in various directions, but we all survived.

Anne van den Bergh became an ardent foxhunter. "I'll never forget as a teenager hacking out of Vernon Manor in the morning mist to hunt with Essex. Today, with the way the area has grown, this would be suicide."

The prefix Vernon appears in the names of not only the stable and Gambrill's beagle pack, but also Gambrill's summer home, Vernon Court, in Newport, Rhode Island. There, Gambrill was a director and president of the golf club and enjoyed time on his yacht, *Carolina*.

Grandson Peter Villa, a well-known dealer in sporting art and the family historian of sorts, feels that the prefix Vernon could trace to the Gambrill family's roots in early nineteenth-century Baltimore, where prominent residences were on Mount Vernon Square.

Gambrill's favorite colors were black and red. The coach in Voss' painting incorporates these colors, and Gambrill's racing silks of the same motif were familiar in steeplechase racing.

The Gambrill equestrian heritage remains. Many of his carriages and sleighs are exhibited at the Shelburne Museum in Vermont; Anne van den Bergh is joint-master of the Tewksbury Foot Bassets, which uses the same territory as formerly hunted by the Vernon Somerset Beagles; Gambrill's great-granddaughters, Antonia and Francesca Villa, compete in horse shows; and great-granddaughter Julia van den Bergh wore Gambrill's black-and-red silks to win the pony race at the Essex Point-to-Point in 2002.

Richard V.N. Gambrill's Vernon Manor Stables

Collection of Nicholas Gambrill Villa, oil on canvas, 28 by 36 inches, 1934

Diana Blair Gambrill and Ann Van Nest Gambrill

Collection of Edith Blair Casey,
oil on canvas, 33 by 38 inches, 1931

Richard V.N. Gambrill's daughters were painted on their hunting ponies, Beaver (left, with Diana) and Pickon (Ann riding sidesaddle), in the courtyard of Vernon Manor Stables. Mr. V., a Sealyham terrier, is in the foreground.

Lucetta Crisp

Collection of Mrs. Northrup R. Knox,
oil on canvas, 18 by 24 inches, 1945

Frank Voss' portrait of Lucetta Crisp, age seventeen, on her hunter Mystery (barn name "Misty"), appeared on the cover of *The Chronicle of the Horse* in August 1947. Alexander Mackay-Smith described the art as "one of Mr. Voss' most striking juvenile portraits." He also wrote that the Crisp family bought Misty as a three-year-old from Richard Kirkpatrick, a well-known horseman in Virginia. At the time, Lucetta was eleven. "Misty had some experience under tack and a slight introduction to polo," Mackay-Smith wrote. "But it was only a smattering of the education she was to receive from the capable hands of her young owner."

Misty and Lucetta hunted with the Meadow Brook Hunt near their home in Glen Head, Long Island, and Misty went along when Lucetta attended Garrison Forest School in Maryland, where they hunted with the Green Spring Valley Hounds. They also were successful competitors in horse shows, and with gas rationing during World War II, Misty contributed by becoming a capable driving horse.

Upon her marriage to Northrup R. Knox of East Aurora, New York, Lucetta commenced hunting with the Genesee Valley Hunt, as well as with the Aiken Hounds when wintering in South Carolina, where three generations of the Knox family have served as masters. Helen Knox — Lucetta's mother-in-law and wife of well-known polo player Seymour H. Knox — was Aiken's master from 1940 to 1945. Lucetta was master from 1956 to 1965, and her daughter, Linda Knox McLean, is the current master. Likewise, Misty had a proud heritage in Aiken. When Lucetta served as huntsman for Aiken's pack, Misty's daughter Mystery Sky was Lucetta's mount.

A Basset at Work

Collection of Mrs. Peyton S. Cochran Jr.,
oil on canvas, 12 by 18 inches, no date

Speculation surrounds the origin of Voss' undated painting, *A Basset at Work*. Some art historians feel it's a study for a finished picture for a client, or, more likely, a gift to a basset owner. Nina Rogers — whose husband, the late Charles R. Rogers, was the founder and huntsman of the Timber Ridge Bassets in Maryland — thinks the painting *may* have been a gift to Jane Fowler Bassett, a neighbor of Voss. Bassett once owned a basset. At any rate, Mrs. Peyton S. Cochran Jr. (known to friends as Jeep) — the founder, master, and huntsman of the Calf Pasture Bassets in Glyndon, Maryland — now owns *A Basset at Work*.

As outlined in *The New Basset Hound* by Mercedes Braun, bassets were bred in France in the 1500s, and the breed's name is a derivation of the French word *bas*, meaning a low thing or dwarf. By the late 1800s, English dog fanciers imported bassets, and it's believed that George Washington owned bassets, given to him by Lafayette following the American Revolution. The American Kennel Club first registered bassets in 1885.

Cochran feels that the American Kennel Club standards for judging bassets are detrimental to the hunting ability of the breed. "The AKC bassets are way too bulky and too close to the ground," she said. "I'll guarantee that the belly of this year's champion at the Westminster Kennel Club Show wouldn't clear the ground by an inch. There's no way he can hunt in the field." As a result, Cochran's breeding program features a cross with the larger, more athletic English bassets, and she imported one from France several years ago. Calf Pasture's crossbred packs have been frequent winners at the Basset Pack Trials in Aldie, Virginia. "I'd love to have a pack of hounds just like the one in my painting," Cochran said. "He's got everything I look for."

A Basset at Work once again indicates Voss' versatility. The painting has great animation, and the impressionistic background helps make the subject stand out.

The Norwich Terrier
Cinnamon

Collection of Moira McLean Hoen,
oil on canvas, 12 by 16 inches, 1946

C innamon, the subject of this canine portrait, was owned by Mr. and Mrs. Edward T. McLean, neighbors of Mr. and Mrs. Dean Bedford and their Pemberton Kennel, a leading breeder of Norwich terriers from the 1920s through the 1950s. It is logical to assume that Cinnamon had Pemberton bloodlines. Like the Bedfords' Napoleon (page 146), Cinnamon was a prick-eared Norwich terrier.

Early in the twentieth century in England, Frank Jones bred the first Norwich terriers. The breed got its name from Jones' home in England and is now also known as the Norfolk terrier. Robert E. Strawbridge, a Pennsylvania sportsman who was the master of the Cottesmore Hunt in England in the early 1920s, brought back one of Jones' terriers. Named Willum, he became a prolific sire.

In addition to the Bedfords and Strawbridge, the leading breeders of Norwich terriers in the United States included fellow foxhunters Constance L. Larrabee and Theodora A. Randolph. Mrs. Larrabee, who bred terriers under the kennel name King's Prevention, was the wife of Sterling Larrabee, founder of the Old Dominion Hounds in Virginia; the accomplishments of Mrs. Randolph, who bred terriers at her Oakley Kennel, are outlined in the foxhunting chapter (page 114).

The Norwich Terrier
Ch. Wychdale
Napoleon

Collection of Muffy Bedford Raines,
oil on canvas, 14 by 18 inches, 1951

C h. Wychdale Napoleon was a foundation sire for Mr. and Mrs. Dean Bedford's Pemberton Kennel, located in Fallston, Maryland. Originally, Norwiches came in two "models," those with prick ears, like Napoleon, and those with drop ears. In 1979 the American Kennel Club recognized prick- and drop-eared terriers as separate breeds, the Norwich and Norfolk respectively.

The Complete Dog Book, an official publication of the AKC, describes the Norwich terrier:

They are hardy, happy-go-lucky, weatherproof companions. Though game on vermin, they are unusually gregarious with children, adults and domestic animals. They weigh about twelve pounds, are short-legged [ten inches maximum at the shoulder], sturdy, and they can be any shade from wheaten to dark red, black, tan or grizzle. They are very loyal, alert and have a sensitive intelligence.

The paintings of Napoleon and Cinnamon are indicative of Voss' mastery of anatomy, be it equine or canine, and we will see on following pages that he could portray poultry just as well.

It's difficult to believe that cock fighting was once an approved pastime of schoolboys, that it was England's national sport for hundreds of years, and that some of the founding fathers of the United States fought chickens.

George Ryley Scott writes in his book, *The History of Cockfighting*, that it was common practice until well into the twelfth century in England for schoolboys to bring gamecocks to school on Shrove Tuesday. A classroom was transformed into a cockpit by removing desks; a schoolmaster supervised the fights. Scott states that a prayer book was awarded the winner at one of these sessions.

By the sixteenth century, cockfighting was taken over by adults, and the sport earned popularity on a par with soccer and horse racing in England today. Often, cockfights were held in conjunction with race meets. All classes enjoyed the sport, and it had the support of royalty. Scott describes the enthusiasm for the sport by Lord Derby, the founder of the Jockey Club and England's premier race, the Epsom Derby, which bears his name:

He was without question the leading cocker of either ancient or modern days … His birds were by judicious breeding brought to the finest possible perfection. It is said that each year he raised no fewer than 3,000 birds.

Frank S. Shy states in his book, *The Claymore*, that cockfighting had been popular in many parts of North America ever since the arrival of the first Europeans. George Washington was active in cockfighting; when Thomas Jefferson built Monticello, he brought fighting chickens with him; Andrew Jackson was accom-panied by racehorses and fighting chickens when he moved from Tennessee to become president.

In 1922 eight proper Bostonians founded the Heel Tap Club, which hosted chicken fighting mains, a series of matches for birds of varying weights. In 1940 an annual tournament, the Claymore, suc-ceeded Heel Tap. Founded by highly respected Massachusetts sports-man Bayard Tuckerman Jr., the Claymore had members well known in a number of fields: Thomas W. Murphy was legendary in harness racing; Lewis Ledyard was a breeder-owner of Thoroughbreds in

Game Cock

Collection of Frank J. Hoen III,
oil on canvas, 12 by 14 inches, 1941

Pennsylvania; Harry A. Parr IV was a member of a family long involved in horse racing in Maryland; James F. McHugh had champion steeplechase horses; and Marion du Pont Scott was the First Lady of both steeplechasing and chicken fighting. Her Virginia estate, Montpelier, was the birthplace of President James Madison. Mrs. Scott converted the car-riage house into an elaborate cockfighting pit.

Today, chicken fighting is illegal in all states except Louisiana. That is not to say, however, that the practice is dead. A veteran chicken fighter, who will remain unnamed, told me that law enforcement officers in his locale look the other way when he has fights so long as there is no wagering, admission, prizes, or the use of liquor. He added that the Claymore is contested to this day.

I can remember in the 1960s when a traditional cockfight on the eve of the Maryland Hunt Cup was raided and permanently shut down. Some forty years later, while in Florida, I was watching the evening news, and images of fighting chickens in the arms of police zipped across the screen, the victims of a crackdown.

Game Hen

Collection of Josiah Lott, oil on canvas,
12 by 16 inches, 1941

Edward T. McLean of Gamecock Farm, Monkton, Maryland, commissioned Voss to paint the portrait of his game hen as well as the game cock on the previous page. Upon becoming an important official at Delaware Park racetrack, McLean retired from cockfighting to avoid possible embarrassment to the track's owners. He traded his birds for a horse. The paintings of the chickens are now in the collections of McLean's grandsons.

Appendix

FRANKLIN B. VOSS BOOK OF ORDERS, 1912–1922
Voss filled commissions for the following in the above years:

Appleton, Charles L.
Arthur Ackerman & Son
Burden, Mrs. Arthur
Burden, Mrs. J.A.
Burke, Carleton
Carhart, A.S.
Cassatt, Capt. E.B.
Clark, F. Ambrose
Clothier, Mr. and Mrs. Isaac H.
Cochran, A.S.
Collins, Henry L.
Dieterich, Mrs. Alfred
Dows, David
Fiske, Charles
Flanagan, Joseph F.
Fleitmann, H.L.
Flint, Dr. and Mrs. Austin
Fowler, Arthur
Gambrill, Richard V.N.
Gerry, Robert L.
Goelet, Robert
Goodwin, Walter L.
Hazard, William A.
Healy, Paul
Higginson, A.H.
Hill, James A.
Horne, Elsa
Iselin, Capt. C. Oliver
Jeffords, Walter M.
Keene, Foxhall P.
Kilmer, W.S.
Langley, William C.

Lewis, Mr. and Mrs. B.B.
Lowe, Mr. and Mrs. W.G.
Meadow Brook Hunt
McLean, E.B.
Milburn, Mrs. Devereux
Munn, Mr. and Mrs. C.A.
Page, Harry S.
Park, James
Riddle, Mr. and Mrs. Samuel D.
Roche, Francis
Ross, Commander J.K.L.
Rutter, Ted
Sanford, John
Schley, Evander B.
Schwartz, A.C.
Schwartz, M.L.
Shaw, James I.
Stoddard, Louis E.
Strawbridge, Robert E.
Thomas, Joseph B.
Thorne, Oakleigh
Von Stade, F.S. (Skiddy)
Webb, J.Watson
White, Windsor
Whitney, Mrs. Payne
Widener, George D.
Widener, Joseph E.
Wilson, Mrs. R.T.
Wing, John D.
Wing, S. Bryce
Winmill, Mrs. R.C.

COMMISSIONS IN 1912

Total commissions in 1912 — $800

Wilson, Mrs. R.T.
Alambala (liver ch. horse), 18 x 24 in., $200
Tommy (white fox terrier), 14 x 16 in., $75
Winchester (pointer), 16 x 22 in., $125
Two pointers, 18 x 24 in., $200
Three fox terriers, 18 x 24 in., $200

COMMISSIONS IN 1913

Total commissions in 1913 — $3,595

Gerry, Robert L.
Gerry in scarlet on Hamsah, 36 x 47 in., $800
Gerry's five-year-old son on gray pony, 12 x 16 in., $150

Appleton, Charles L.
Mr. Appleton in Mrs. Whitney's colors on Webb Carter, 22 x 27 in., $400

Wing, John D.
Bay hunter Aberdeen, 16 x 22 in., $100

Lewis, B.B.
Chestnut hunter Shamrock, 16 x 22 in., $200

Hill, James A.
Watercolor of steeplechase at Belmont Terminal, 14 x 24 in., $50

Thorne, Oakleigh
Brown hunter Ardsley, 18 x 24 in., $200

Dieterich, Mrs. Alfred
Mrs. Dieterich on Arlington, 36 x 47 in., $800
"Paid in installments of $200, $250, $100, and $250"

Clark, F. Ambrose
Bay hunter Night Hawk with the Scotty, Toby, 18 x 24 in., $250
Hunter Sally Coombs, 18 x 24 in., $250
Chestnut hunter with fox terrier, 18 x 24 in., $250

Hazard, William A.
Lamp shade (watercolor) of international polo, $35
Set of 18 china plates, $20 each, $360

COMMISSIONS IN 1914

Total commissions in 1914 — $2,000

Wilson, Mrs. R.T.
Marion on Shetland pony, $300
Louisa on buckskin pony, $300
Mr. Wilson with two pointers, $350

Webb, J. Watson
Bay hunter Los Alamos, 18 x 24 in., $200

Lewis, Mr. & Mrs. B.B.
Sealyham terrier Punch, owned by E.H. Carle, 24 x 30 in., $200

Cassatt, Capt. E.B.
Racehorse Flying Fairy, L. Davis up, 24 x 30 in., $500

Healy, Paul
Portrait of Paul Healy, described by Voss as "son of S. H.,"
small canvas, $100

Higginson, A. Henry
Foxhound Middlesex Ranger, 20 x 27 in., $200

Appleton, C.L.
Mrs. Payne Whitney's steeplechase horse Cherry Malotte, 18 x 24 in., $200

Page, Harry S.
Steeplechase horse Gold Plate, 18 x 24 in., $100

COMMISSIONS IN 1915

Total commissions in 1915 — $3,219

Burden, Mrs. J.A.
The field hunter Craven, 18 x 24 in., $250
Painted at Westbury, Long Island, New York

Keene, Foxhall P.
Steeplechase horse Toreador, Keene up, 22 x 32 in., $400
Painted at Hewlett, L.I., NY

Park, James
Steeplechase horse Duke of Halmuth, 18 x 24 in., $200
Painted at Belmont Park

Roche, Francis
   White pony Snowball, 20 x 24 in., $300. Painted at Newport, RI

Sanford, John
   Bay horse The Curragh, 23 x 32 in., $400. Painted at Amsterdam, NY

Gambrill, R.V.N.
   Two sketches of beagles, $25 each. Painted at Newport, RI

Schwartz, A.C.
   Mr. Schwartz on polo pony Bushwacker, 23 x 32 in., $500
   Painted at Babylon, L.I., NY

Schwartz, M.L.
   Portrait of Jeffy, 18 x 24 in., $200. Painted at Babylon, L.I., NY

Webb, J. Watson
   Chestnut horse Allenadale, 18 x 24 in., $200
   Hunter Octagon, 18 x 24 in., $200
   Hunter Quaker Girl, 18 x 24 in., $200
   Two sketches of English foxhounds, $50 each. Painted at Shelburne, Vt.

Burden, Mrs. J.A.
   Sketch of black spaniel, $50

Von Stade, F.S.; John D. Wing; J. Kane; and Mrs. Burden
   Candle shades, a total of $169

COMMISSIONS IN 1916
Total commissions in 1916 — $8,050

Dows, David
   In scarlet coat on hunter Butwell, 23 x 32 in., $500
   Painted at Old Westbury, L.I., NY

Wilson, Mrs. R.T.
   Sketch of fox terrier's head, $75. Noted, "Not paid."

Schwartz, M.L.
   Portrait of St.Patrick, 20 x 25 in., $250
   Painted at Roslyn, L.I., NY

Von Stade, F.S.
   Bay hunter Justinian, 19 x 24 in., $250
   Sketch of brown pony, $100
   Painted at Old Westbury, L.I., NY

Goelet, Robert

Ogden Goelet on bay pony with black dog. Lake in distance, 22 x 30 in., $700

Peter Goelet on brown pony with two dogs, a Bull Terrier and a West Highland, 22 x 30 in., $700

Painted at Goshen, NY

Burden, Mrs. Arthur

Portrait of chestnut hunter Sarah Maude, 20 x 24 in., $250

Painted at Brookville, L.I., NY

Goodwin, Walter L.

Portraits of polo ponies Bonnie and Do-Do, 16 x 22 in., $200 each

Portraits of hunters Hidden Treasure and Good Night, 18 x 24 in., $200 each. Painted at Hartford, Conn.

Milburn, Mrs. Devereux

Portrait of chestnut polo pony Teuby, 18 x 24 in., $250

Painted at H.P. Whitney's stables

Rutter, Ted

Sketch of Billy, a West Highland, $75

Painted at Glen Cove, L.I., NY

Wilson, Mrs. R.T.

Ches. colt Campfire, J. McTaggart up, after winning the Futurity, $1,000

Jeffords, Walter M.

Gray hunter Long Point, the property of S.D. Riddle, 22 x 32 in., $600

Mrs. Jeffords on chestnut hunter Dr. McCaughran, 32 x 44 in., $1,000

Painted at Glen Riddle, Penn.

Riddle, Mrs. Samuel D.

Portrait of dog Totty, 18 x 20 in., $200

Painted at Glen Riddle, Penn.

Fowler, Arthur

Portrait of Mrs. Fowler on roan hunter Gambler, 22 x 32 in., $600

Painted at Peapack, New Jersey

Meadow Brook Hunt, presentation portrait

H.I. Nicholas, MFH, with huntsman, whip, and hounds, 28 x 40 in., $700

Painted in Meadow Brook country

COMMISSIONS IN 1917
Total commissions in 1917 — $4,775

Schwartz, M.L.:
  Portrait of racehorse N. J. Shannon, 22 x 32 in., $600

Fiske, Charles
  Portrait of Foxy Foot from photo, 12 x 16 in., $75
  "Given to James Brady"

Schley, Evander B.
  Portrait of Penhurst Mischief Maker, an Ayreshire bull, $300
  Portrait of The Whip, a black hunter, $300
  Portrait of Tipperary Boy, a bay hunter, $300

Kilmer, W.S.
  Portrait of Sun Briar in stall, 22 x 32 in., $600
  Painted at Binghamton, NY

Riddle, Samuel D.
  Portrait of Mr. Riddle's hounds with MFH, huntsman, and whips
  leaving the kennels, $2,000. Painted at Glen Riddle, Penn.
  Sketches of three horses, $200 each

COMMISSIONS IN 1918
This was sole commission listed for 1918

Kilmer, W.S.
  Portrait of Sun Briar, 31 x 43 in., $1,200
  Painted at Saratoga, Aug. 21-28

COMMISSIONS IN 1919
Total commissions in 1919 — $16,750

Thomas, Joseph B.
  Paintings of six hunting countries "for reproducing." $2,000
  Piedmont — "Full Cry" and "Leaving the Kennel"
  Meadow Brook
  Millbrook
  Essex
  Harford   "Piedmont to belong to J.B.T., the other 4 to me."

Iselin, Capt. C. Oliver
Sketch of the beagle Chancellor, $50

Stoddard, Louis E.
Portraits of 4 polo ponies in stalls, $300 each

Shaw, James I.
Portrait of polo pony Kamano, 18 x 24 in., $300

Milburn, Mrs. Devereux
Portrait of polo pony Jacob, 18 x 24 in., $300

Lowe, W.G.
Portraits of three hunters in stalls, 16 x 22 in., $300 each
Portrait of daughter on hunter, 16 x 22 in., $800

Cochran, A.S.
Portrait of Ethel Frank in stall, 16 x 22 in., $300

Webb, J. Watson
Portraits of 4 ponies, $1,200
Portraits of 4 terriers, $600

Strawbridge, Robert E.
Portrait of pony, $300

Two others on page 41 of the order book are too faint to read at $300 each

Ross, Commander J.K.L.
Sir Barton with Loftus up, 30 x 40 in., $1,000
Billy Kelly with Sande up, 30 x 40 in., $1,000
Cudgel with Sande up, 30 x 40 in., $1,000
All three painted at Saratoga

Riddle, S.D.
Man o' War with Loftus up, 30 x 40 in., $1,000. Painted at Berlin, Md.

Lowe, Mrs. W.G.
Mrs. Lowe on The Rook, $1,000

Collins, Henry L.
Chestnut stallion Guigo, 18 x 24 in., $600

Widener, Joseph E.
Portrait of Naturalist, 16 x 22 in., $700

Munn, Mrs. C.A.
Mrs. Munn on Salisbury, 26 x 34 in., $1,000
Fox terrier head, 10 x 12 in., $200

Widener, George D.
  Lausonis, 16 x 22 in., $700

COMMISSIONS IN 1920
Total commissions in 1920 — $5,700

Burke, Carleton
  Portrait of polo pony Scottie, 16 x 22 in., $350
  Portrait of Patti Amaca on The Stern
  and given to Mrs. Mather, 24 x 32 in., $1,000
  Sketches of The Stern made at Cleveland, Ohio

White, Windsor
  Portrait of hunter Halfbred, 16 x 20 in., $700
  Painted at Cleveland

Strawbridge, Robert E.
  Portrait of polo pony Sanora, 16 x 20 in., $350

McLean, E.B.
  Portrait of The Porter at Saratoga, 24 x 32 in., $800
  Portrait of The Porter with Butwell up, $1,200

Stoddard, Louis E.
  Portrait of Devereux Milburn on Jacob, 28 x 36 in., $800

Arthur Ackerman & Son
  Portrait of Man o' War, C. Kummer up, for aquatint, 22 x 29 in., $500

COMMISSIONS IN 1921
Total commissions in 1921 — $6,200

Langley, William C.
  Mrs. Langley on Sandown, $1,000

Munn, C.A.
  Sketch of Peter Grey, 14 x 18 in., $200

Clothier, Mrs. Isaac H.
  Sir Lucien at Devon, Penn. 18 x 24 in., $600

Von Stade, F.S.
  Skiddy Jr. on chestnut pony, 18 x 22 in., $500

Ross, Commander J.K.L.
  Milkmaid in stall, 16 x 22 in., $800

Fleitmann, H.L.
Painting of Joshua in stall, "in exchange for Sealyham terrier Rags and $100."

Lowe, Mrs. W.G.
Portrait of Mrs. Lowe on Rosy O'Mara, 28 x 36 in., $1,000

Thorne, Oakleigh
E.H. Carle on Runway, 28 x 36 in., $1,000

Flint, Dr. and Mrs. Austin
Dr. & Mrs. Flint on Big Brother and Bennington, 26 x 34 in., $1,000

COMMISSIONS IN 1922
Total commissions in 1922 — $14,300

Horne, Elsa (future sister-in-law)
Portrait of Gray Eagle in stall, 18 x 24 in., $400

Gambrill, R.V.N.
Portrait of brown hunter in stall with Sealyham terrier, 18 x 24 in., $400

Webb, J. Watson
Portrait of English foxhound Rundle, 14 x 18 in., $200

Riddle, S.D.
Head study of Dream of the Valley, 10 x 12 in., $100

Wedding present to Edward S. Voss
Portrait of Malagash, 18 x 24 in.

Flanagan, Joseph F.
Portrait of Lytle in stall, 18 x 24 in., $400

Kilmer, W.S.
Portrait of Exterminator, 16 x 22 in., $700

Wedding present to Elsa Horne Voss
Portrait of the whippet Kelly, 16 x 20 in.

Langley, William C.
Painting of Meadow Brook Hunt crossing Underhill's farm, Jericho, L.I., 18 x 24 in., $500

Clothier, Isaac H. Jr.
Portrait of Catherine Clothier on bay pony with wire-haired terrier, 22 x 30 in., $600

Winmill, Mrs. R.C.

Mr. & Mrs. Winmill on Oliver (gray) and Serf, 28 x 36 in., $1,200

Additional fee of $300 for change of horses in picture

Whitney, Mrs. Payne

Portrait of Cherry Pie, 18 x 24 in., $700

Painting of Syosset, ridden by Powers, jumping at Belmont Terminal, 24 x 30 in., $800

Sanford, John

Laddie Sanford on polo pony Lavender, 26 x 34 in., $1,000

Higginson, A.H.

Mr. Higginson's hounds in the Millbrook country, 16 x 24 in., $500

Webb, J. Watson

Mr. Webb on Vulture with five English hounds, 28 x 36 in., $1,600

Carhart, A.S.

Gray hunter in stall, 16 x 22 in., $400

Burden, Mrs. James A.

Meadow Brook hounds and field on the lawn of "Woodside," Mrs. Burden's estate at Syosset, L.I., 32 x 42 in., $3,000

Wing, S. Bryce

Portrait of Mrs. Wing on chestnut hunter, walking, 28 x 36 in., $1,000

Riddle, S.D.

Painting of Mr. Riddle's hounds leaving the kennel at Glen Riddle, 16 x 24 in., $500

Books of Order have not been found for subsequent years.

VOSS PAINTINGS ON THE COVER OF
THE CHRONICLE OF THE HORSE MAGAZINE

1/31/47 — Stuart S. Janney on Winton

8/8/47 — Mahmoud, Leading Juvenile Sire

8/15/47 — Lucetta Crisp on Mystery

9/26/47 — Peterborough,
J. Stanley Reeve's Irish Cob

10/29/48 — Mr. Stewart's Cheshire Foxhounds

12/3/48 — J. Stanley Reeve on Peterborough

12/2/49 — Mrs. Tyson Gilpin on Forest King

4/7/50 — Dr. A.C. Randolph

10/20/50 — Elkridge-Harford Hunt's meet at St. James Church

6/8/51 — Thomas Allison on Pickle

10/19/51 — George Humphrey on Richmond Boy

3/7/52 — Huntsman Blowing Hounds Away

3/14/52 — Dallas Leith, Huntsman of the Elkridge-Harford Hunt

5/23/52 — Owen J. Toland's Justa Boy

6/13/52 — Greentree Farm's Capot at Pimlico

7/18/52 — Louise Lott Bedford of Maryland

12/19/52 — George D. Widener's Eight Thirty

8/14/53 — Julia and Cherry Ripe
(for Arthur Pew Jr.)

9/25/53— J. Watson Webb's Hound, Heythrop

4/30/54 — Harry Webb's horse Alan-A-Dale

5/28/54 — J. Watson Webb's International Polo Ponies

6/18/54 — William Voss on Wizard

1/14/55 — The stallion Roman

1/24/58 — Tally-Ho (Bryce Wing viewing
fox away at Millbrook, NY)

3/24/61 — Sally Combs (F.A. Clark Collection)

6/2/61 — J. Stanley Reeve

4/24/64 — Coaching with F. Ambrose Clark

7/12/68 — Man o' War as a Two-Year-Old

2/14/69 — W. Plunket Stewart

7/2/71 — Howard Bruce on Billy Barton

4/16/76 — International Polo, 1924

9/15/83 — Night Hawk (F.A. Clark Collection)

9/18/92 — Working It Out

7/8/94 — Mrs. J.H. Whitney on Grey Knight

5/12/95 — Paul Mellon's Welbourne Jake

5/10/96 — Howard Bruce on Billy Barton
(same as 7/2/71)

5/11/01 — Alligator

9/21/01 — Thomas Allison on Pickle
(same as 6/8/51)

PAINTINGS BY EDWARD S. VOSS
ON THE *CHRONICLE'S* COVER

9/15/50 — The Harford Fox

2/9/51 — Great Steeplechase Horse Elkridge

12/21/51 — In Full Cry

4/29/77 — Third Fence in the Maryland Hunt Cup

Acknowledgments

The author is indebted to the following institutions and persons:

The National Sporting Library, where an incredible collection of books enabled the author to research the subjects in the Voss paintings;

the archives of *The Blood-Horse*, *The Chronicle of the Horse*, and *Mid-Atlantic Thoroughbred* magazines and the Keeneland Library;

Lori A. Fisher, Curator of Collections of the National Museum of Racing and Hall of Fame, for her support of the book from its inception;

F. Turner Reuter Jr. of Red Fox Fine Art (Middleburg, Virginia), Greg Ladd of Cross Gate Gallery (Lexington, Kentucky), and Peter L. Villa of Peter L. Villa Fine Art (New York City) for advice and for helping to locate paintings, in many cases providing transparencies of paintings for reproduction in this book;

Margaret H. Whitfield for valuable editorial advice;

Mr. and Mrs. Thomas H. Voss for support of the undertaking throughout;

Peyton S. Cochran Jr. for assembling sixty-five Voss paintings for an exhibition at the Museum of Hounds & Hunting in Virginia in 1999;

William Voss Elder, Patrick Smithwick, and Sybil K. Dukehart for information on the Voss and Neilson families;

Brandon Webster for photographing many of the paintings;

Mary W. Winants for encouragement and understanding;

Jacqueline Duke and her associates at Eclipse Press for vital contributions in the publishing and marketing processes.

About the Author

For many years Peter Winants, a native of Maryland, photographed horses for advertising purposes and took pictures of horse racing and other horse sports for various magazines. In 1972 he joined the staff of *The Chronicle of the Horse*, a national weekly magazine based in Virginia, and, in time, became the editor, then publisher. After retiring from the *Chronicle* in 1991 at age sixty-five, Winants became the director of the National Sporting Library in Middleburg, Virginia, for nine years. He is now director emeritus of the library, which has one of the world's largest collections of books on horses, horsemanship, and associated field sports.

Winants' first book, published by Winants Brothers Inc. in 1966, concerned the American steeplechase horse Jay Trump, who won the 1965 English Grand National. In 1989 Winants authored the biography of steeplechase champion Flatterer, published by *The Chronicle of the Horse*. Derrydale Press published Winants' *Steeplechasing: A Complete History of the Sport in North America* in 2000 and *Foxhunting with Melvin Poe* in 2002. *The Sporting Art of Franklin B. Voss* is Winants' fifth book.

Winants resides in Rectortown, Virginia, near Middleburg.